JEFFERSON
THE FORGOTTEN MAN

Th: Jefferson

JEFFERSON
THE FORGOTTEN MAN

by

SAMUEL B. PETTENGILL

MEMBER OF CONGRESS

with a foreword by

DOUGLAS JOHNSON

Author of *"The Assault on the Supreme Court"*

In Cloth—$1.50
In Paper—$1.00

Published by
AMERICA'S FUTURE, INC.
205 EAST 42ND STREET
NEW YORK, N. Y.

PRINTED IN THE UNITED STATES OF AMERICA
BY J. J. LITTLE AND IVES COMPANY, NEW YORK

 199

Dedicated To

JEFFERSONIAN DEMOCRATS AND
LINCOLN REPUBLICANS

*"Soberly it is now no child's play
to save the principles of Thomas
Jefferson from total overthrow in
this nation."*

A. LINCOLN

PREFACE

On the afternoon of July 4, 1826, the 50th anniversary of the Declaration of Independence, couriers spurred their horses down the slopes of Monticello. As they proceeded to Richmond, Charleston, Washington, Philadelphia, New York, Boston and to the tiny hamlets hid between ocean and wilderness, the newspapers, day by day, in ever-widening circle, carried the headlines "Jefferson is Dead".

The news travelled slowly. There was no telephone, no telegraph, no radio. It did not reach John Adams. The second president was also destined to die on the same day—a coincidence which, as it became known, seemed like a Divine portent. Adams, up in Massachusetts, on this 4th of July 1826, was thinking of those who had signed the great Declaration in the prime of a golden youth, 50 years ago. He whispered, "Jefferson still lives," and crossed the dark frontier to immortality.

A few days later at Monticello, on the hill slope Jefferson had climbed so often, shaded by trees he loved, a stone slab was laid, inscribed with these words written by the man himself:

"Here was buried

Thomas Jefferson

Author of the

Declaration of American Independence

of

The Statute of Virginia for Religious Freedom

and

Father of the University of Virginia."

But despite these proofs of his passing, for over a century they were never wholly believed. A great political party did not accept them. Millions of other Americans rejected them. They refused to believe that the essence of Jefferson, that which made him *Jefferson,* and without which the man would now be nameless and forgotten, the principles he fought for, and the truths he taught, had been buried beneath the slab.

There have been times when this faith of his friends has been shaken. One of these friends was Abraham Lincoln. Only 33 years later Lincoln said, "The principles of Jefferson are the definitions and axioms of a free society, and yet they are denied and evaded, with no small show of success."

A generation later Senator George F. Hoar of Massachusetts recognized that men sometimes wander from his teaching but held "the perfect assurance that on any question of liberty, if the opinion of Thomas Jefferson stand on one side and the opinion of mankind on the other, the world will, in the end, come around to his way of thinking."

Still later Andrew J. Montague, Governor of Virginia, and my well loved colleague in Congress, was also certain that "The political philosophy of Mr. Jefferson will take care of itself. . . . If Mr. Jefferson is wrong, America is wrong. If America is right, Jefferson is right."

We come to 1938. We return to the city by the Potomac where Jefferson was the first president to swear to protect and defend constitutional government, its separation of powers, its checks and balances, and we find these checks and balances slightingly referred to by an assistant attorney general of the United States as "gadgets," and we find many other men using many other words!

We are led to ask if any part of Jefferson has escaped mortality. The "axioms of a free society" are sneeringly described as belonging to the "horse and buggy days." "These expressions, differing in form, are identical in object and effect, the supplanting of the principles of free government." Such was Lincoln's description of similar sneers at Jefferson in 1859.

Still the question remains. In fact, with the single possible exception of the insanity that men call war, the most serious of all questions facing America and the masses of mankind everywhere is whether *Jefferson still lives.*

Samuel B. Pettengill

Washington, D. C.
September 1938.

CONTENTS

FOREWORD

In the year 1932 the American people faced a crisis of the first magnitude. For three years economic conditions in the country had been going from bad to worse—and the worse was very bad. What the worst might soon be, people dreaded to contemplate. Millions of Democrats were ready to support any leader able to repulse those forces of ruin threatening to overwhelm the nation with disaster. Samuel B. Pettengill was one of those Democrats. Millions of Republicans, utterly discouraged by the short-sightedness of party leaders who clung obstinately to policies morally and politically bankrupt, were ready to vote for any man who would lead the country to safety. The writer of this foreword was one of those Republicans.

Then came the voice of one crying in the wilderness. In accents rich and full of compassion it promised the people salvation. With a courage that inspired hope, and a confidence that begat trust, it pledged a new order in government. Reckless spending of the people's money would cease. Special favors to selected groups would end. Squandering of federal income on discredited economic panaceas would be stopped. Overlapping federal bureaus would be consolidated. Useless bureaus would be eliminated. Economy in administration would be inaugurated. The national budget would be balanced. The dangerous trend toward centralization of authority at Washington would be arrested. The FORGOTTEN MAN would be remembered, and the power of government transferred from the privileged few to the hands of all the people.

The people listened, believed, and followed. Democrats and Republicans united in an overwhelming vote to entrust to the new leader the safety of the country. With vigor and courage he attacked the nation's problems. To cope with immediate emergencies he recommended in rapid succession a series of drastic but temporary measures; and Congress as rapidly adopted them. That he might act the more quickly and with greater efficiency he asked for unprecedented grants of power; and these powers Congress placed in his hands. To prevent the recurrence of similar crises in the future, permanent legislation of high value was formulated and enacted into law. The new leader was justifying the confidence placed in him by the people, and Republicans and Democrats alike joined in applauding measures obviously calculated to benefit the country. In the enactment of these measures Congressman Pettengill played an important part.

Then something happened. The letters spelling N E W L E A D E R were shifted about, and the N E W D E A L E R began to play the leading rôle at Washington. Economy flashed in the pan, and reckless expenditures began to mount to heights previously unknown in the nation's peace-time history. Taxes paid by all the people were poured out in unearned bounties to special groups. Discredited economic panaceas won new favor and new defenders. All pretense at balancing the budget was abandoned, and a stupendous debt piled up to crush the people and their children by future taxation. One by one experienced and cautious advisers were dismissed. Clever young radicals gained influence over the inner councils of the nation. In place of consolidation and elimination of federal bureaus, one saw these multiplied in number and magnified in authority. War began to be waged, not only against the *evils* of business, but against private enterprise itself. Government, instead of being decentralized and returned to the people, was transferred to a vast bureaucracy in Washington controlled by a single man. Powers granted by the people for the duration of an emergency were not returned to the people when the emergency ended. On the contrary, powers belonging to Congress and to the

Judiciary were demanded by the new executive as being essential to the attainment of New Deal objectives. Fundamental changes in the people's government were effected without the people's consent.

All this Mr. Pettengill saw from the inside. A loyal Democrat and devoted follower of the New Leader, he helped to uphold the latter's hands in coping with the abuses of special privilege and the selfishness of big business. When the people's New Leader began to change into the political New Dealer, he continued to follow, but with a troubled mind. Nor did he abate allegiance to the titular head of his party until the most fundamental of all issues was squarely raised. This was the issue between subservient loyalty to a chief who had abandoned the teachings of his party and the pledges of its platform, and loyalty to one's own conscience and to the constitution he had sworn to uphold. With that issue before him, Mr. Pettengill did not hesitate. Before the day ended on that fateful February 5th, 1937, he announced he would fight the court-packing bill. He took his stand with the ever-increasing number of distinguished Democrats who from the Vice-President down have thrown their influence on the side of maintaining those principles of constitutional free government which Jefferson and Lincoln so ably defended; and against any impairment of the American system of checks and balances without which, as Washington warned, our government cannot long survive.

One need not hold Mr. Pettengill's political faith to read with interest and with profit what he has written in these pages. But surely every Democrat who cherishes the traditions of his party, and reveres the memory of Jefferson, has special reason to follow the author as he unfolds the story of the unprecedented transformation that has taken place in Washington. On the other hand, Republicans can learn much from this unprejudiced and clear-sighted appraisal of the fundamental principles of our democracy by a Democratic Congressman.

Every American who believes that loyalty to country comes before loyalty to party leaders must find inspiration in the confession of faith of a public servant who in notable degree has acted on this belief.

The reading of Mr. Pettengill's volume should bring Jefferson Democrats and Lincoln Republicans closer together. It should inspire constitutional Democrats and constitutional Republicans to join in protecting our priceless heritage of freedom under a written Constitution. It should reveal to conservative Democrats and liberal Republicans how much they have in common, and make clear the futility of worshipping party labels which have long since lost meaning.

If, by doing these things it impels all Americans who believe in conserving what has proved good and truly liberal in our institutions, to mobilize their combined strength against those who mistake radicalism for liberalism, change for progress, and force for efficiency, then will this book have served the nation well.

Douglas Johnson

88 Morningside Drive,
New York City.

JEFFERSON
THE FORGOTTEN MAN

CHAPTER I

THE NEW DEAL

"It is proper to take alarm at the first experiment upon our liberties. We hold this prudent jealousy to be the first duty of citizens. . . . The freemen of America did not wait until usurped power had strengthened itself by exercise and entangled the question in precedents. They saw all the consequences in the principle and they avoided the consequences by denying the principle."

—James Madison.

Let me say at once that I am certain America will never go back to the Old Deal of frenzied finance, speculation, and the abuse of public trust both in public office and in private life which crashed in 1929. Let me say also that I am for so much of the New Deal as is constitutional, Jeffersonian, and within the nation's pocketbook.

Ardent New Dealers will say that this commits one to all of it as they will not admit any part of it is outside these limitations. Opponents will say that only a small part of the New Deal comes within these boundaries.

There is difficulty in defining the New Deal. The phrase first came into use in 1932. Many of us thought then that the definition of the New Deal was the Democratic platform of that year. That platform was essentially Jeffersonian. Since then we have gone on to what some persons call the Second, or the Third New Deal. I was a New Dealer in 1932 when the New Deal was Jeffersonian. But as it has moved away from the principles of Jefferson to the principles of a centralized government, which would concentrate power at Washington far beyond the dreams of Alexander Hamilton, honest doubts have arisen as to the wisdom of the present trend.

Many people say that the only alternative to the Second or Third New Deal is the Old Deal which fell into ruins in 1929. I do not consider the Old Deal the alternative. The alternative is the first New Deal. It is liberalism. It is the free society conceived by Thomas Jefferson and Abraham Lincoln.

When I reflect upon the enormous burden President Roosevelt is carrying, I have nothing but sympathy for an overworked and stout-hearted man.

He has done two very great things for his country. In the dark days of 1933 his cheerful courage restored the morale of a panic-stricken people. And he has made us alive to the plight of those who live "on the other side of the tracks." If he has failed in this, the fault is ours, not his. For these things, whether Republican or Democrat, we owe him much and few are so unfair as to withhold a generous appreciation.

But, as the French express it, "Every man has the defects of his virtues." This is true of the President. In the spring of 1933 his sense of the dramatic, his courage, his improvisations, his "quarterback" theory served the nation well. We were ready "to try anything once" and the "applause of listening Senates to command" was his in heaping measure.

But there were implied conditions to the applause. It was given to meet an emergency, to meet a situation we hoped was temporary. It was given to legislation which contained time limitations which would shortly bring the legislation to an end. It was given further with the assurance that if mistakes were made they would be openly acknowledged; if laws failed to work they would be abandoned.

But now the nation is leveling off for the long pull, or trying to. We are settling into harness. Five years have gone by and the sixth has begun. The dramatic quality no longer serves. We no longer want the "quarterback" to call strange signals, and we certainly do not want the rules changed constantly. We want continuity and stability instead. We want, in short, the opposite of what we wanted in 1933. Business today wants to be able to see ahead and chart its course.

Until the second crash in 1937 we had a certain species of prosperity. It was a prosperity in the buying of gasoline, and rayon stockings, and tobacco, and motion picture tickets. It was based on short range confidence. It was a prosperity in consumers' goods only. At no time since 1929 have we had a prosperity in durable goods, in houses, locomotives, utility construction, heavy machinery, factory buildings. In all these things we have done scarcely half as well as we did in 1923-4-5 when we had 16,000,000 fewer Americans to do such things for.

And what is the reason for this? It is that we have not had a long range confidence. A young married couple have spent money for gasoline but not to build a house. Prosperity in durable goods requires a confidence and sense of security in future events lasting more than thirty days. This we have not had.

One reason for this is that an uneasy feeling has grown up as "emergency" expedients adopted in 1933 and 1934 now unroll as permanent programs involving a profound break with the past. Many, like myself, who warmly supported the President in 1933, have begun to ask "Where are we going?" and "Is it necessary to go that far?" We see our children swept on in a strange current to unknown rapids. We are afraid we shall lose them.

The "break" came February 5, 1937, when the President startled the nation with his disingenuous and ill-starred plan to pack the Supreme Court and to create a "flying squadron" of hand-picked judges to go here and there throughout the land to try—and convict—American citizens. That was supported by the plea that we did not have time to amend the Constitution; that the people might not agree to amend it anyhow even if requested; and therefore we must amend it anyway, with or without the "consent of the governed."

The people like a certain amount of clever politics. But when the men in the jury box get the idea that the plaintiff's attorney is "getting too smart"—watch out. They lose confidence in the plaintiff's case when they lose confidence in the plaintiff's attorney.

But this was not all. There was the enormous concentration of power in Washington and the concentration of this power in fewer and fewer hands. We saw the Reorganization Bill in 1937 to subject the independent commisions, such as the Interstate Commerce Commission, to the will of the President. We saw the pyramid of popular sovereignty gradually turned to rest upon its apex. We saw sovereign states with hat in hand asking Washington for money to shingle a schoolhouse. We saw Congressmen and Senators pushed around by smart young sophomores who never carried a precinct or met a payroll. We saw an incredible confusion and contradiction of purpose. We saw the power to "regulate the value of money" transferred from Congress to the Executive. We saw farmers directed from Washington "when to sow and when to reap." We saw the affairs of the smallest factory in the hands of unknown agents of a distant government. We saw citizens become mendicants with tin cups in their hands held out to Washington. We saw public expenditures grow. We saw the public debt mount and mount to totals never heretofore dreamed of in times of peace. We saw the government year after year, now for the ninth consecutive year, pledging the earnings of the future to meet present expenditures, robbing the children's bank to fill the pay envelopes of today. We have seen all this despite repeated promises that "next year" we would live within our means, that we would balance our budget. We have begun to ask whether our children can pay their debts and ours besides.

And, then, we began to become aware that in the turmoil

and confusion, we had somehow reversed the course of 150 years,—that what we were doing and the direction of our going was away from the teachings of Jefferson.

The most profound lesson of history is that the life habits of a people are hard to break; that they cling desperately to the legacies of the past; that they discard but slowly the methods their fathers used.

This is especially true of a free people. But it is true even of a people without liberty. The Russians, for example, are finding this out today. Even the French Revolution, the most violent wrench from old grooves of thought the world has ever known, passed over France and except in Paris left practically no mark on the daily lives and habits of its people.

For these reasons we are now taking inventory. Item by item we are going over our inheritance, appraising the present and weighing the future. And as we do so we ask, is it true that little of the past is worth saving? We read our first president's Farewell Address and ask ourselves "Has General Washington failed us?" Has Lincoln's dream proved worthless? Is Thomas Jefferson dead?

CHAPTER 2

OBJECTIVES VERSUS METHODS

The objectives of the New Deal, First, Second or Third, have been often stated and widely discussed. Probably no one has better summarized the first New Deal, at least, than President Roosevelt did on June 10, 1935, when he said—

"The social objective (of the administration) I should say remains just what it was, which is to do what any honest government of any country would do; to try to increase the security and the happiness of a larger number of people in all occupations of life and in all parts of the country; to get them more of the good things of life, to get them a greater distribution of not only wealth in the narrow terms, but of wealth in the wider terms; to give them places to go in the summer time—recreation; to give them assurance that they are not going to starve in their old age; to give honest business a chance to go ahead and make a reasonable profit, and to give everyone a chance to earn a living."

This is the New Deal at its best, and the President at his best,—with the possible exception of the emphasis on the word "give," as if any government can "give" its people the good things of life. Surely these are objectives which all decent men must approve. It is simply and nobly said. There is no patent medicine in it.

Another definition of the New Deal and its objectives was given by Senator Edward R. Burke of Nebraska in the campaign of 1934, and warmly endorsed by the President. Senator Burke stated it as follows:

"The 'new deal' is an old deal—as old as the earliest aspirations of humanity for liberty and justice and the good life. It is old as Christian ethics, for basically its ethics are the same. It is new as the Declaration of Independence was new, and the Constitution of the United States. Its motives are the same; it voices the deathless cry of good men and good women for the opportunity to live and work in freedom, the right to be secure in their homes and in the fruits of their labor, the power to protect themselves against the ruthless and the cunning. It recognizes that man is indeed his brother's keeper, insists that the laborer is worthy of his hire, demands that justice shall rule the mighty as well as the weak. It seeks to cement our society —rich and poor, manual workers and brain workers—into a voluntary brotherhood of free men, standing together, for the common good of all."

We have here two statements of the "objectives" of the New Deal which are worthy to live. God speed the day when these definitions become realities!

But it is precisely at this point that we must recognize, as the President said, that the objective is "what any honest government of any country would do." In short, the stated objectives of his administration are the objectives of any honest administration anywhere. Or, as Senator Burke said,—its motives are the same as Christian ethics and the Declaration of Independence.

It is for this reason that it ought not to be possible longer to divide our people into warring camps over objectives. What were the objectives of Thomas Jefferson? They were set forth in his first inaugural address as follows:

"What more is necessary to make us a happy and prosperous people? Still one thing more, fellow-citizens, a wise and frugal government which shall restrain men from injuring one another, which shall leave them otherwise free to regulate their own pursuits of industry and employment and shall not take from the mouth of labor the bread that it has earned. . . . Equal and exact justice to all men. . . . Economy in public expense that labor may be lightly burdened; the honest payment of our debts and the sacred preservation of the public faith; encouragement of agriculture, and of commerce, its handmaid; the diffusion of information and the arraignment of all abuses at the bar of public reason; freedom of religion; freedom of the press; . . . these principles formed the bright constellation which has gone before us. . . . They should be the creed of our political faith; the text of civil instruction; the touchstone by which to try the service of those we trust."

These historic phrases have been household words for 137 years as the definition of the very soul of America, the fighting faith of the great liberal who moulded the thought of the nation "when men grew tall."

When we consider these "objectives" of Roosevelt and the "creed" of Jefferson we can find no substantial difference. There is none.

It should now be plain that such differences as exist between Jeffersonian Democrats and Lincoln Republicans on the one hand, and New Dealers on the other, are not differences of objectives.

They are *differences of methods*.

It is here that the public mind has been confused. Our citizens have been persuaded, almost bludgeoned into believing that if they agreed on "objectives" they must "go along" on any and all methods. They have been told that if they did not accept the methods they were traitors to the objectives. They were "not social minded," they were "selfish," "tories," "economic royalists," "Neanderthalers," "dead cats," "copperheads," etc., etc.

But methods are important and men cannot be driven from the temple of democracy because they honestly differ on ways and means.

What is democracy anyway but a method? What is constitutional government but a method? What are "state rights" but a method? What is Congress but a method? What is the Supreme Court but a method? What is the separation of powers between the executive, legislative and judicial branches of government, but a method?

In short, what is the difference between constitutional democracy and the totalitarian state, if it is not precisely a difference in method? Both profess the "same objectives" and probably with equal sincerity. All dictators profess to desire happiness and prosperity for their people. Most dictators in fact claim that their governments are supremely effective in promoting the public good. However much we may dislike them and their methods, it is entirely possible that Hitler, Mussolini, and Stalin are as sincere in trying to serve their people as any president who has tried to serve our people.

One can, indeed, accept the professed "objectives" of Hitler, Mussolini, and Stalin and yet disagree violently with the methods by which they seek to obtain these objectives.

The time has surely come in America when we should stop trying to divide our people over objectives. Without taking exception to the objectives of President Roosevelt, as above quoted, there are many of us who believe that certain of his methods are not "liberal" but are in fact Tory and reactionary. On these points the next chapter will offer evidence. It treats of France in the days before the Revolution, and shows clearly that many methods of government then in vogue have their counterpart today.

We will go farther and more safely if we use the methods of Jefferson when pursuing the objectives of Roosevelt and Jefferson.

Since writing the foregoing, one of the wisest men of our times, Brandeis, said to me, "Methods are all we are sure of."

CHAPTER 3

"THE NEW DEAL"—"THE OLD REGIME"

So let us discuss "methods." It will be found that certain methods urged today have their counterpart in the past—a past that Jefferson rejected.

These precedents may be found in the history of many centuries. With them Jefferson had a profound acquaintance. Their development in England led to the great Declaration of 1776. Here the "objective" was "Life, Liberty and the pursuit of Happiness." The break with England took place because the "*form* of Government" became "destructive of these *ends*."

Methods and forms were important to Thomas Jefferson. He did not believe liberal ends could be attained by illiberal means, nor a democratic result by a dictatorial method.

We will return again to England's colonial policy. For the moment let us consider conditions in France which preceded the Terror of the 1790's, the beginnings of which Jefferson saw with his own eyes during his five years' residence there as Minister, 1784-1789.

Our authority is the great Frenchman, Alexis de Tocqueville, (author of the famous "Democracy in America") in his book on his own country, "The Old Regime and the Revolution." The following paragraphs are from this notable book. Please observe that it was written in 1856, or eighty-two years ago. This absolves it of any charge of bias or partisanship in today's politics. Nevertheless these paragraphs seem like items from the daily papers.

"The law obliged no man to take care of the poor in the rural districts; the central government boldly assumed charge of them."

"Not content with aiding the peasantry in times of distress, the central government undertook to teach them the art of growing rich, by giving them good advice, and occasionally by resorting to compulsory methods."

"Orders were passed prohibiting the cultivation of this or that agricultural produce in lands which the Council considered unsuited to it. Others required that vines planted in what the Council regarded as bad soil should be uprooted. To such an extent had the government exchanged the duties of sovereign for those of guardian."

"Some reduction of the burdens which weighed on agriculture would probably have proved more efficacious; but this was never contemplated for a moment."

"You have neither Parliament, nor estates, nor governors; nothing but thirty masters of requests, on whom, so far as the provinces are concerned, welfare or misery, plenty or want, entirely depend."

"The government had a hand in the management of all the cities in the kingdom, great and small. It was consulted on all subjects, and gave decided opinions on all; it even regulated festivals. It was the government which gave orders for public rejoicing, fireworks, and illuminations."

"Municipal officers were impressed with a suitable consciousness of their nonentity."

"The church, which a storm had unroofed, or the presbytery wall which was falling to pieces, could not be repaired without a decree of Council. This rule applied with equal force to all parishes, however distant from the capital. I have seen a petition from a parish to the Council praying to be allowed to spend twenty-five livres."

"Under the old regime, as in our own day, neither city, nor borough, nor village, nor hamlet, however small, nor hospital, nor church, nor convent, nor college, could exercise a free will in its private affairs, or administer its property as it thought best. Then, as now, the administration was the guardian of the whole French people; insolence had not yet invented the name, but the thing was already in existence."

"Ministers are overloaded with business details. Everything is done by them or through them, and if their information be not coextensive with their power, they are forced to let their clerks act as they please, and become the real masters of the country," (the bureaucracy of the 18th Century).

"Judges whose position was beyond the king's reach, whom he could neither dismiss, nor displace, nor promote, and over whom he had no hold either by ambition or by fear, soon proved inconvenient," (as they did in 1937).

"A very extensive machinery was requisite before the government could know every thing and manage every thing at Paris" (just as at Washington!). "The amount of documents filed was enormous, and the slowness with which public business was transacted such that I have been unable to discover any case in which a village obtained permission to raise its church steeple or repair its presbytery in less than a year. Generally speaking, two or three years elapsed before such petitions were granted," (the modern name is "red tape").

"A marked characteristic of the French government, even in those days, was the hatred it bore to every one, whether noble or not, who presumed to meddle with public affairs without its knowledge. It took fright at the organization of the least public body which ventured to exist without permission. It was disturbed by the formation of any free society. It could brook no association but such as it had arbitrarily formed, and over which it presided. Even manufacturing companies displeased it. In a word, it objected to people looking over their own concerns, and preferred general inertia to rivalry."

"It seldom undertook, or soon abandoned projects of useful reform which demanded perseverance and energy, but it was incessantly engaged in altering the laws. Repose was never known in its domain. New rules followed each other with such bewildering rapidity that its agents never knew which to obey of the multifarious commands they received."

"Nobody expected to succeed in any enterprise unless the state helped him. Farmers, who, as a class, are generally stubborn and indocile, were led to believe that the backwardness of agriculture was due to the lack of advice and aid from the government." (How familiar this sounds!)

"Government having assumed the place of Providence, people naturally invoked its aid for their private wants. Heaps of petitions were received from persons who wanted their petty private ends served, always for the public good."

"Sad reading, this: Farmers begging to be reimbursed the value of lost cattle or horses; men in easy circumstances begging a loan to enable them to work their land to more advantage; manufacturers begging for monopolies to crush out competition; business men confiding their pecuniary embarrassments to the intendant, and begging for assistance or a loan. It would appear that the public funds were liable to be used in this way."

"The local franchises of the rural districts were fading away, all symptoms of independent vigor were vanishing, provincial characteristics were being effaced, the last flicker of the old national life was dying out."

"France is nothing but Paris and a few distant provinces which Paris has not yet had time to swallow up."

All this de Tocqueville says in 1856, adds up to the following:

"History, it is easily perceived, is a picture-gallery containing a host of copies and very few originals."

So much from the great Frenchman writing of his own land under the Old Regime. Change "Paris" to "Washington," "provinces" to "states" and "France" to "the United States," and de Tocqueville has painted with marvelous precision our country in the year 1938.

Now let us turn to Jefferson, who was in France immediately following our own Revolution of 1776 and just before the French Revolution broke out. What did Jefferson think of all this as he went from house to house, observing the life of the rich and the poor, looking in their kitchens and kettles to see what they had to eat and asking how much they produced, what taxes they paid, what lives they lived. I quote what he said:—

"Never was there a country (France) where the practice of governing too much had taken deeper root and done more mischief."

"As for France and England with all their preeminence in science, the one is a den of robbers, the other of pirates."

"Nor should we wonder at the pressure (for a fixed constitution in France in 1788-9) when we consider the monstrous abuses of power under which these people were ground to powder, the enormous expenses of the Queen, the Princes and the Court, the shackles on industry by guilds and corporations."

"It is urged principally against the King that his revenue is one hundred and thirty millions more than that of his predecessor and yet he demands one hundred and twenty millions further."

"The consternation is as yet too great to let us judge of the issue. It will probably ripen the public mind to the necessity of a change in their constitution and to the substituting the collected wisdom of the whole in place of a single will by which they had been hitherto governed. It is remarkable proof of the total incompetency of a single head to govern the nation well, when, with a revenue of six hundred millions they are led to a declared bankruptcy, and to stop the wheels of government even in its essential movements, for want of money."

"You have heard of the peril into which the French Revolution is brought by the flight of their King. Such are the fruits of that form of government which heaps importance on idiots and of which the tories of the present day are trying to preach into our favor."

Jefferson believed as a cardinal principle of government that it should be decentralized. He had witnessed at first hand both at home and in France the evils, the abuses, and the dangers of a concentrated government. Whatever justifications may be urged in favor of concentration, then or now, it must be plain that no one can defend it on the ground that it is Jeffersonian. The doctrine of a concentrated government looking after the most minute affairs of the States from a central bureaucracy, is as far from the teachings of Jefferson as the North Pole is from the South.

Such was the regimentation of the 18th century, known to economists as "mercantilism," and to others as paternalism. It is often supposed that government was simple "in the good old days"; that it was simple because no other kind was necessary, and that centralization of control and bureaucratic regimentation at the nation's capital has existed only since, and only because of, the "economic integration" of the network of radios, railroads, telegraphs, fast-moving transport, and all the paraphernalia of modern science and technology.

The contrary is the truth. The itch to govern is an ancient and hereditary disease and laid its heavy hand on the simplest affairs of the smallest village two centuries ago.

"I have myself counted in a provincial town of no great size in the year 1750, the names of 109 persons engaged in administering justice, and 126 more busy in executing their orders."

de Tocqueville

It was a similar flock of human locusts coming from England who were described by Jefferson as "swarms of officers to harass our people and eat out their substance."

Nor is it true as is so often supposed that the modern octopus of a soulless corporation stretching its tentacles over a vast empire is a creature spawned only by the industrial revolution. The contrary is true. It is probable that few, if any, modern corporations occupy in their respective fields a monopoly as rigid or over as great a territory as the Hudson Bay Company, the South Sea Company, the Dutch East India Company, the

West India Company, and others of the 16th and 17th centuries.

There were giants in those days as now. They were giants for the reason, often, that they purchased the powers of government. There was also the tanglefoot of a sticky bureaucracy. Big and small, the problems of today are neither new nor peculiar, except in their application. It is a serious mistake to put Jefferson and his colleagues in the discard on the assumption that they "failed to anticipate" these modern problems. They knew about them and had, because of their knowledge, as little use for state monopoly as business monopoly.

CHAPTER 4

WHY DID JEFFERSON REVOLT?

"Restrain men from injuring one another but leave them otherwise free to follow their own pursuits of industry and employment."

—Jefferson's first inaugural,

Why did our forefathers take the momentous step of declaring their independence from the mother country? Why did Jefferson write the great Declaration?

The Revolutionary War was not of religious origin. It was not a dynastic revolt. Many, including George Washington, declared their affection for the Crown. It was primarily an economic rebellion against official intermeddling in business.

It was a war of independence against too much government. It was an armed protest against a distant government that tried to build up one industry, or one part of the empire, or one class of people, at the expense of some other. No doubt it was justified in debate as "for the good of the empire," or for the "general welfare" or other sonorous phrases with which legislation is decorated by pressure groups.

1776 is one of the very few periods in human history in which men "played over their heads" to use an athletic term. In that year the great Declaration of Independence was written. In that same year Adam Smith's "Wealth of Nations" came from the press, challenging for the first time the old doctrine that one man's gain is another man's loss, and so revolutionizing economics.

Only seven years before, James Watt was puzzling his brain over the hidden giant whose shoulder was moving the lid of the teakettle. So, in a period of a very few years we saw new beginnings of political freedom, of economic freedom, and the birth of the age of steam, which brought on the industrial revolution. In looking back upon it, it is no wonder that we speak of it as a time "when men grew tall."

A few years later the French Revolution broke out and whatever its excesses and crimes, it also marked the liberation of men's minds from old superstitions, political and economic.

It was an age which challenged the mercantilism of the Middle Ages. This was a philosophy of a planned economy in which government, and government officials, undertook to tell men not only what they could *not* do but what they *must* do. It was to free themselves from the restrictions placed upon them and upon their business and commerce by the government of England that our fathers declared their independence.

The great historian, John Fiske, says—

"In one of its most important aspects the Revolution was a deadly blow, aimed at the old system of trade restriction."

The Declaration declared war against these restrictions. And the Constitution which followed thirteen years later, furnished safeguards against their return. These two documents dedicated America to private enterprise, and freed it from collectivism. Those, therefore, who would today control the most minute affairs of our people would turn the clock back to pre-Revolutionary time. Believing the Constitution antiquated, they want something still more antiquated.

Let us see the picture as Jefferson saw it. One hundred and twenty-five years before the Declaration, in 1651, the British Parliament passed a Navigation Act. This required that all colonial products exported to England must be carried in ships of British origin and manned by British sailors. It was the first step in a program designed to restrict the commercial development of one part of the empire for the benefit of another part. Nine years later, the Navigation Act of 1660 was passed.

This required that all colonial goods shipped to foreign buyers must first land their cargoes in England. This gave English manufacturers the first choice of the cargoes as well as the handling and insurance charges on re-export.

In the same year, New England fish were excluded from English markets for the benefit of English fishermen. Still later, other staple products of New England and the Eastern Seaboard, such as wheat, corn, flour and meat were barred from English markets. These restrictions automatically served to curtail production. It was a sort of AAA.

In addition, when attempting to limit what the colonies might produce, the British planners also attempted to control what the colonists might consume. If they bought in foreign countries the imports must be carried on British ships and pass through British ports, so that English ship owners, manufacturers and merchants might profit. The importation of products directly from European nations was prohibited. The Colonial Duty Act of 1673 was designed to give the cargo insurance to British insurers.

But not only were restrictions placed upon the movement of goods across the Atlantic; in addition, restrictions were placed upon manufacturing in the colonies for the benefit of British manufacturers. This was an imperial NRA. As early as 1699 the export of American wool, yarn and cloth was forbidden. In 1732 the House of Commons created a commission which found that "great quantities of hats" were being manufactured in New England and were being exported to the West Indies, Spain and Portugal. The English hatmakers asked for a law to prevent it, and Parliament gave them the law. The exportation of hats from the colonies to foreign buyers was prohibited. This gave British hatmakers the foreign market.

In the effort to restrict production in the colonies labor provisions were enacted. For example, the number of apprentices was limited to two to a master hatmaker, and an apprenticeship of seven years was required. This, of course, was to prevent too many hats from being made and to prevent too many working-men going into business.

English iron and steel manufacturers naturally did not want the processing of iron to take place in the colonies. So, in 1717 the English smiths and iron workers petitioned Parliament for protection against iron processors in the colonies. Parliament very obligingly granted their request and a law was passed forbidding the erection in the colonies of any mills or machinery to process iron. By royal proclamation of 1763, fur trading west of the Alleghenies was forbidden except by royal license. This, of course, favored the Hudson Bay Company and English fur dealers, but it was tough on the colonies.

The Molasses Act of 1733 was passed by Parliament to prevent Americans from buying molasses except from the *British* West Indies. This, of course, destroyed their trade with foreign countries and gave the British Indies a monopoly of the American molasses business.

The Sugar Act of 1764 prohibited the importation of rum, or spirits, from foreign plantations and placed an increased duty on imports of foreign sugar. This Act ruined the trade of the colonies with the West Indies and contributed heavily to the growing antagonism of the colonists.

A planning board was set up at London, where all authority over the colonies was centralized, known as the "Board of Trade and Plantations." It had general supervision over all economic activities in the colonies. In regard to this organization, Professor Charles A. Beard writes—

"Until the eve of the Revolution this Board kept all American affairs drawn tightly within its dragnet (note the word), holding five meetings a week during most of its career and in periods of relaxation eight or ten sessions a month. If an English merchant or manufacturer had a plan or suggestion to make about the acts of any colonial authority, or about methods to control American industry, he could find a sympathetic hearing before the Board of Trade."

This "Board of Trade and Plantations" was a sort of AAA, NRA and Wage-Hour affair, designed to protect profits, stabilize industry, favor one part of an industry or one set of workmen as against another. It operated also as a limitation of production to enhance prices paid by consumers.

And so a long series of Acts of Parliament and edicts from the Board of Trade and Plantations, growing cumulatively, and beginning with fish in 1651, went on to include corn, flour, meat, wool, yarn, woolen cloth, hats, bar and pig iron, sugar, molasses (shades of Tugwell!), rum, spirits, tobacco, cotton, indigo, ginger, tar, pitch, hemp, turpentine, ship masts and yards, rye, beaver skins, copper and iron ore, hides, whale fins, silk, lumber, dye woods, finally winding up with tea, then the Tea Party in Boston Harbor and the shot heard 'round the world!

Benjamin Franklin was a solid and substantial citizen. He was not by temperament a flaming revolutionary. But all this effort on the part of government to regulate business provoked the old philosopher to say—

"It is of no importance to the common welfare of the empire whether a subject of the King obtains his living by making hats on this side or that side of the ocean. Yet the hatters of England have prevailed to obtain an Act in their own favor restricting that manufacture in America. In the same manner that a few nail makers and a still smaller batch of steel makers, perhaps there are not half-a-dozen of these in England, prevail totally to forbid by an Act of Parliament, the erection of slitting or steel furnaces in America."

How reminiscent this all is of some recent efforts to allocate production, restrict credit, and prevent competition against an established industry, as well as the direct prohibition of new factory building, as in the NRA Furniture Code.

Such was the "invisible government" of the 1700's. A modern counterpart is the Sugar Quota Bill of 1937 which allocated the refining of sugar to different refiners; a measure, I am glad to say, President Roosevelt is said to have opposed, although he signed the bill, and with respect to which the writer was one of his few supporters in the House of Representatives.

By July 4, 1776, the colonists had had all they wanted of economic planning by their competitors. On that day they tore these throttling hands from the throat of American commerce, industry and agriculture. "A long train of abuses" borne with "patient sufferings" and all "having in direct object the establishment of an absolute Tyranny over these States" were "submitted to a candid world."

Among them were:

"Cutting off our Trade with all parts of the world. . . ."
"Imposing Taxes upon us without consent. . . ."
"He has made Judges dependent on his Will alone. . . ."
"He has sent hither swarms of Officers to . . . eat out our substance."
"Taking away our Charters, abolishing our most valuable Laws, and altering fundamentally the Forms of our Governments."
"Suspending our own Legislature, and declaring themselves invested with power to legislate for us in all cases whatsoever."

And so it was solemnly published and declared that

"These United Colonies are, and of Right ought to be Free and Independent States."

Years later, writing about the events that led up to the Revolution, Jefferson said—

"Sound heads saw in the first moment that he who could put down the loom, could stop the spinning wheel, and he who could stop the spinning wheel could tie the hands that turned it. Who were to be judges whether duties were imposed with a view to burden and stress a branch of manufacture or to raise a revenue?"

A few more of his observations will further illustrate that this was his settled view:

"I own I am not a friend of a very energetic government. It is always oppressive. It places the governors indeed more at their ease at the expense of the people."

"The ultimate powers of government extend to such acts only as are injurious to others."

"I think, myself, that we have more machinery of government than is necessary, too many parasites living on the labor of the industrious. I think it might be much simplified to the relief of those who maintain it."

"The system into which the United States wished to go was that of freeing commerce from every shackle."

"The trade of the Colonies was laid under such restrictions as show what hopes they might form from the justice of a British Parliament were its uncontrolled power admitted over these states."

"Surely under such a mass of misrule and oppression a people might justly press for a thorough reformation and might even dismount their rough-shod riders and leave them walk on their own legs."

"Nor should we wonder at this pressure when we consider the monstrous abuse of power under which these people were ground to powder. When we pass in review the weight of their taxes, the oppression of the tithes, the shackles on commerce by monopolies, on industry by Guilds and Corporations. . . ."

Such was the "invisible government" seizing economic power in legislative halls. It was this that caused Jefferson to revolt.

CHAPTER 5

LINCOLN AND JEFFERSON

"The principles of Jefferson are the definitions and axioms of a free society."

—Abraham Lincoln.

It is easier to read labels than analyze contents. The result is that long after the contents have been adulterated, we keep right on buying—the label. In the field of politics we call this process party loyalty—loyalty to a label. This loyalty is commendable only if the contents are loyal to the label. Abraham Lincoln once described a political contest as two men engaging in a fight, throwing their coats on the ground, and after they had fought sufficiently they often left the field of honor each wearing his opponent's coat and claiming it as his own.

In the less important business of foods and drugs we have laws against using labels that falsely describe the contents. In the field of public affairs, however, the rule is "caveat emptor!" —Let the buyer beware.

The men who founded this republic had time to think. We seldom do. On his journey to Philadelphia in 1797 to become Vice-President, Jefferson spent five or six days on the road from Monticello. The same journey today takes but a few hours.

Lincoln was 17 years old when Jefferson died. Lincoln also had time to think. Each of them took time to analyze contents as well as read labels. And they were more interested in contents than in labels. Party names were changing rapidly in the first half century of our national life. But the accepted principles of government changed very little if at all.

24

Principles are still important. They are more important now, in fact, to 130 million people than they were to Jefferson and Lincoln with only a few million people. And despite the pressures of modern life there are still those who do care about principles. They are in both of the great parties today. This chapter is for the men and women of both parties who still believe in the institutions which made this country great.

(The struggle to preserve our constitutional democracy and system of free enterprise and to prevent its being engulfed by collectivist philosophy is going to require the support of all such men and women.)

The title given this book might at first blush appear intended only for those who have been known as Democrats. The contrary is the case. If we will read not only the labels but examine the contents we will find that the Republican as well as the Democratic party is historically rooted in the teachings of Jefferson. It is only this label worship and the expediencies of politics which have obscured the truth.

Abraham Lincoln was a political first cousin of Thomas Jefferson. He believed in freedom more than in authority. I have never run across any tribute paid by Abraham Lincoln to Alexander Hamilton, the apostle of centralization. On the other hand Lincoln repeatedly acknowledged his indebtedness to Jefferson. It was not until the imperialism following the Spanish American War, with its slogans of "manifest destiny" and "the new nationalism" that Theodore Roosevelt, Elihu Root and others promoted Hamilton as the patron saint of the Republican party.

A spokesman for the Republican party has recently said, "I would not have you believe that the Republican party always has been faithful to the principles of Jefferson which constituted the political faith of Lincoln. There have been periods in our history when the Republican party has slipped away from these principles and has followed strange gods. But whenever the Republican party has departed from basic Jeffersonian principles, it has not been true to itself."

The same might be said of the Democratic party. As a matter of fact Lincoln did say so in April 1859. He had been invited to attend a celebration in Boston in honor of the birthday of Thomas Jefferson. Although unable to come, Lincoln sent to that meeting a testimonial in which he argued that his own party now stood where Jefferson had stood and Jefferson's party occupied a position contrary to the ideals of its founder. To use his exact words, Lincoln wrote on that occasion:

"Bearing in mind that about seventy years ago two great political parties were first formed in this country (i. e. Federalist and anti-Federalist) that Thomas Jefferson was the head of one of them and Boston the headquarters of the other, it is both curious and interesting that those supposed to descend politically from the party opposed to Jefferson should now be celebrating his birthday in their own original seat of empire, while those claiming political descent from him have nearly ceased to breathe his name anywhere.

"Remembering, too, that the Jefferson party was formed upon its supposed superior devotion to the personal rights of men, holding the rights of property to be secondary only, and greatly inferior, and assuming that the so-called Democracy of today are the Jefferson, and their opponents anti-Jefferson party, it will be equally interesting to note how completely the two have changed hands as to the principle upon which they were originally supposed to be divided. . . ."

What Lincoln wrote on that occasion cannot be attributed alone to the fact it was only a year before he was nominated by the new Republican party for the office of President of the United States. A dozen years before Lincoln had served one term in Congress and in two speeches made by him in the House of Representatives, he spoke of Thomas Jefferson and his principles in highly complimentary terms.

In 1852 Mr. Lincoln was asked to deliver an eulogy on Henry Clay and at the close of his address he read a long letter by Jefferson which he felt to be complimentary to the subject of the address. In his famous debates with Stephen A. Douglas, when they were both candidates for the Senate, Lincoln again and again sustained his argument by quoting from Jefferson.

The Republican party made its first campaign in 1856. Lincoln had been a candidate for the nomination as Vice-President upon the ticket. The party platform of that year dedicated the party to "restoring the action of the federal government to the principles of Washington and Jefferson." And resolved—

"That the maintenance of the principles promulgated in the Declaration of Independence and embodied in the Federal Constitution are essential to the preservation of our republican institutions, and that the Federal Constitution, the rights of the States, and the Union of the States must be preserved."

One of its distinguished founders said at the time—

"There is not a plank in our platform which does not conform to the principles of Jefferson, the man who, of all others, has ever been regarded as the true representative of the republican party of this country. . . . We stand, sir, upon his doctrines and we fight for his principles. We are coming to take possession of this Government, to administer it for the whole country, and shall suffer monopolists neither of the North or South to control its administration and so shape its action as to subserve the interests of the aristocratic few."

This same plank was repeated four years later in 1860 when Lincoln was nominated. Still four years later, in 1864, Abraham Lincoln ran for reelection not on the "Republican" ticket but the "Union" ticket; his running mate being an anti-slavery Southern Democrat, Andrew Johnson of Tennessee.

The name "Republican" by which the new party went forth

to war in 1856 was the same name as the Democratic Party had borne when Jefferson, Madison and Monroe won their great victories. It was in truth founded by a coalition of Whigs and Free-soil Democrats who had kept faith with the teachings of Jefferson, who in writing the Declaration of Independence, had attempted to obtain a prohibition against slavery and who, in the other great document of which he was the author, the Ordinance of 1787 for the Government of the Northwest Territory, had provided—

> "There shall be neither slavery nor involuntary servitude in the said Territory otherwise than in the punishment of crimes."

This famous document, by the way, ante-dated the drafting and ratification of the Constitution of the United States which made its famous compromise with slavery.

It was entirely consistent therefore in its first campaign in 1856, for the new Republican Party, having named John C. Fremont for president, to adopt as its campaign slogan the words, "free speech, free press, free land, free men, and Fremont."

Referring again to the letter which Lincoln wrote to the Boston dinner in honor of Jefferson in 1859, he further said,

> "Soberly, it is now no child's play to save the principles of Jefferson from total overthrow in this nation. . . . The principles of Jefferson are the definitions and axioms of a free society. And yet they are denied and evaded with no small show of success. One dashingly calls them 'glittering generalities.' Another bluntly calls them 'self-evident lies.' And others insidiously argue that they apply to 'superior races.' These expressions, differing in form, are identical in object and effect—the supplanting the principles of free government, and restoring those of classification, caste and legitimacy. They would delight a convocation of crowned heads plotting against the people. They are the vanguard, the miners and sappers of returning despotism.

"We must repulse them or they will subjugate us. This is a world of compensation; and he who would be no slave must consent to have no slave. Those who deny freedom to others deserve it not for themselves, and, under a just God, cannot long retain it. All honor to Jefferson—to the man who, in the concrete pressure of a struggle for national independence by a single people, had the coolness, foresight, and capacity to introduce into a purely revolutionary document an abstract truth, applicable to all men and all times, and so to embalm it there that today and in all coming days it shall be a rebuke and a stumbling-block to the very harbingers of reappearing tyranny and oppression."

From all of this it is clear that it was only after Lincoln had groped his dark way to a martyr's tomb that the party of which he was the chief founder, during the tragic days of reconstruction, and later yielding to the pressure of the manufacturing North for high tariffs, and to the new nationalism following the war with Spain, gradually and by degrees almost imperceptible to its adherents, left its first moorings, abandoned its primary loyalty to Jefferson, and gradually embraced the aristocratic and centralizing teachings of Alexander Hamilton.

In the light of this historic record, I find no inconsistency whatever as a Jeffersonian Democrat, in asking those of my readers who are Republicans to join in rededicating America to the faith of the men who founded both of the two great parties.

A like argument made eight years ago fell under the eye of the great historian of Jefferson and Hamilton, Hon. Claude G. Bowers, Ambassador to Spain. Under date of January 15, 1931, Mr. Bowers was kind enough to write me as follows—

"I have just read with interest and enthusiastic approval your speech in the Record on Lincoln. You are absolutely sound of course in your history, and most effective in making the point that the Republican party of today is the party of Hamilton and not of Lincoln who was a Jeffersonian. In my latest book on 'The Tragic Era' I think I make it clear how the party of Lincoln was taken over by the Hamiltonians."

From Lincoln to the lobbyists of special privilege the distance is as great as that between "a certain rich man" and Lazarus in the bosom of Abraham. Between them "there is a great gulf fixed." But when one goes from the grave at Monticello to the shrine at Springfield, it is as if one were visiting the same God's acre where all his forebears sleep.

But Lincoln is not the only Republican to pay tribute to Jefferson. Other men high in the councils of that party have done the same,—Calvin Coolidge, Charles Evans Hughes, many others. But regardless of the passing incidents which have in years gone by formed points of disagreement, those today who still believe in free enterprise as against collectivism, in liberty as against bureaucracy, and in the historic separation of powers between the nation and the states, will find in both Jefferson and Lincoln sufficient to justify the "faith of the fathers."

CHAPTER 6

THE LAW OF THE PENDULUM

No one can read history without becoming aware of the "Law of the Pendulum."

1. We go to extremes.
2. We go from Pollyanna to Gloomy Gus.
3. We plot enough lots in Florida for every house in America.
4. We buy at the top and sell at the bottom.
5. Mr. Hoover carries all states but eight; four years later he loses all states but six.
6. We write success stories about the "captains of industry." Then a decade later the business man is a hissing and a byword among the nations.

One year we worship anybody who has a million dollars, *no matter how he got it*. The next year the only person who has wisdom or virtue, is the man with holes in the seat of his pants. If he has nothing, he knows everything.

Politicians know the law of the pendulum and ride it to their advantage. Depending upon what party is in power they always give it too much credit or too much blame. They point with pride or view with alarm. In doing so, the thinking of the nation is always carried beyond the point to which it will ultimately return.

At the present time we are shell-shocked by the depression. Fears haunt us and hopes hypnotize us. In trying to rid ourselves of the evils of Big Business we are embracing the evils of Big Government. Our illusion today is that we *must* center practically all power in Washington, however much we regret doing so.

We are told that commerce, industry, business, agriculture, banking, has become a single thing, a "seamless web," an "economic unit," and therefore must be regulated, if at all, only at a single point.

Day by day we are told that our problems are "national," made so by the growing interdependence of the moving parts of our economic machine. We are told, or it is implied, that city, county, and state legislators and officials are incompetent or corrupt. That business is "selfish," "without vision." That disinterested wisdom dwells only in Washington, and it is only federal politicians who are paragons of virtue.

Such is the law of the pendulum.

Nevertheless, we must face honestly the questions that have arisen in the mass thinking of the nation. We must not run away from realities, even on the hobby horse of "state rights." While our argument is that the trend towards centralized government is dangerous, and that most of it is wholly unnecessary, no Jeffersonian is under obligation to shut his eyes to things as they are.

Jefferson himself did not do so. Jefferson did not ride a hobby to death, nor must we. Identified as he is as the great protagonist of—

"The support of the state governments in all their rights as the most competent administrations for our domestic concerns and the surest bulwarks against anti-republican (Fascist) principles."

He declared, with equal force, in his first inaugural address, for

"The preservation of the General government in its whole constitutional vigor as the sheet anchor of our peace at home and safety abroad."

Let us get this straight. No Jeffersonian is precluded from advocating national remedies for national problems, if

(a) The problem *is* national,

(b) If it can be solved effectively only by national action, and

(c) If the national remedy does not create more new problems and greater difficulties than it attempts to cure, as, for example, Federal prohibition.

Whatever our approach to the problems of today by either national, state, or local methods, we should keep in mind the words of wise old Benjamin Franklin—"Don't pay too much for your whistle."

It is not necessary now, however, to argue the cause of nationalism. Too many powerful voices are doing that today to need our help. Our responsibility it is to recognize this "law of the pendulum" and not be swept too far from ancient landmarks by the totalitarian tide.

It may help to rouse us from our present trance if we ask ourselves, very honestly, what caused the debacle of 1929. At the present moment the accepted doctrine seems to be that it was due to inherent and incurable defects in our system of constitutional government and private enterprise. We will readily agree that there were many causes for that debacle and we may differ among ourselves not only in what they were but the weight to be assigned to each of them.

Admittedly there are national problems created by the development of science and technology, which require national solutions, even if those solutions are as new as our science. For example, federal control of radio communication. Radio waves do not stop at state lines and from that fact it is perfectly clear that for each of the 48 states to attempt to regulate radio transmission would deprive any broadcaster of a free air channel. We would have the same confusion and traffic jams in the air as if we were attempting to direct automobile traffic at a busy intersection, by 48 policemen rather than one. In addition the "Old Counsellor" could continue to sell bogus securities to greedy people by radio.

The common sense of the nation has therefore taken federal control of radio communication in its stride, even though we recognize the political dangers inherent in having this control centered at a single point.

Admittedly, too, reform was long overdue in 1933 in the interstate sale of stocks and bonds, in the divorcement of deposit from investment banking, in the management of the stock exchanges, the regulation of interstate electric light and power utilities, clearing the jungle of pyramided holding companies, putting brakes upon over-speculation, and in other matters important to the business health of the nation. While some of this new legislation and the regulations issued under it probably went too far, and have harmfully restricted the flow of capital, nevertheless, reform along these lines in 1933 was necessary and was entirely within the Jeffersonian principle to—

"restrain men from injuring one another."

Few today deny that these reforms were needed and few withhold from President Roosevelt credit for the courage to sponsor them.

Nevertheless it is necessary to come back to the fundamental question whether the crash of 1929 was due to any inherent and incurable defects in our system of constitutional government and free enterprise. A candid survey of the events leading up to that crash points to the conclusion that it was due more to the mistakes made *by government,* and particularly by the *federal government,* than to business which is today in the doghouse.

If that crash was due to the post-war tariffs and the reprisals they provoked abroad, depressing agricultural sections at home, the mistake was made *at Washington.* It was a mistake of the federal government.

If it was due to over-speculation and debt—it was officially encouraged *at Washington.*

If it was due to the assurance that we had attained a "new

and permanent plateau of prosperity," that assurance was given *at Washington*.

If it was due to a faulty monetary system, the fault lay *at Washington*.

If it was due to a defective banking and credit system, it was the fault of government, the national government with respect to national banks, and the state governments, with respect to state banks.

If the World War was a horrible mistake, it was a mistake of government. And if our participation in it was a mistake, it was the mistake of our own government *at Washington*.

If, following the World War, the reduction, four times repeated, of income taxes on the high brackets caused over-expansion, over-speculation, and the diversion of the nation's wealth into concentrated pools of vast private fortunes, the reductions took place *at Washington*.

If post-war loans to foreign buyers to buy our goods—which was the same as giving the goods away—resulted in inevitable collapse, the loans were made or encouraged—*at Washington*.

If the failure to enforce the Sherman Anti-trust Act or to amend it permitted monopoly to drive small business to the wall, the failure took place *at Washington*.

But why go on? Some of the fault, certainly, was back in the states. I have already mentioned one—defective regulation and inspection of state banks. Another was too loose state legislation with respect to granting charters to corporations, to holding companies, and with respect to wild cat stock issues, and their sale.

Enough has been said, however, to demonstrate that Washington, D. C., has the major responsibility for the great depression, insofar as its contributing causes originated on American soil. The depression was not due to the Constitution of the United States, nor free enterprise, and no one even suggested it until a year ago. It was not due to our governmental checks and balances, the separation of power between the legislative, executive and judicial branches of government. It was not due to the Supreme Court or to any decision of the Nine Old Men. It was not due to the absence of one-man government.

It was due, in large part, to mistakes of government officials. But it was not due to our *system* of government. The mistakes can be corrected, but nothing points to the necessity of scrapping the Constitution; wiping out the states; making Congress a rubber-stamp; or making the President ex-officio Chief Justice of the Supreme Court of the United States.

Prior to the crash, the free enterprise system had been engaged in the age-old problem of production. It had come closer to solving that problem than during all of the centuries of the past. It had brought us out of an economy of scarcity for the first time in human history to the actual possibility of an economy of plenty. Engrossed with this gigantic task our free enterprise system and its managers had not solved so well the secondary problem of distribution. There is, however, no evidence that there is any defect inherent in the system of private enterprise that will prevent finding a solution for the problem of distribution, as it has already so nearly found the answers to the primary problems of production. In fact—it *must* solve the distribution problem. Production is meaningless unless it is done.

But, because our business structure did collapse and politicians led us to believe that it was due chiefly to the faults of business, rather than to the mistakes of government, we have chosen the wrong remedy. We are engaged today in the *most minute* control of business. In doing so, we are turning the pyramid of government more and more to rest upon its apex, rather than upon its base. We do so in the name of security. But a pyramid, resting upon the apex of one-man decision, is not secure, even though that man be the ablest and the most patriotic in the world's history.

We have, throughout the centuries, had plenty of experience of governments resting upon their apexes. We have been duly

warned of the danger of centering power at a single point and
not by Jefferson alone:—

> "We have built up new instruments of public power. In
> the hands of a people's government this power is wholesome
> and proper. But in the hands of political puppets of an
> economic autocracy these powers would provide shackles
> for the liberties of the people."

This warning was given by President Roosevelt and it is as
true as sunshine. But officials need not be base to be dangerous.
Danger also is to be found in well-meant incompetence; in
overloading the human machine with tasks beyond its strength,
with problems beyond its grasp, with pressures it cannot resist,
with donations to party war chests that create inescapable obli-
gations, whether they come from business lobbies or labor
leaders.

My authority for all this is President Roosevelt when he was
Governor Roosevelt. Sounder Jeffersonian doctrine was never
preached by any citizen since Jefferson, than by Mr. Roosevelt
in 1930.

> "Were it possible to find master minds, so unselfish, so
> willing to decide unhesitatingly against their own personal
> interests or private prejudices, men almost godlike in their
> ability to hold the scales of justice with an even hand,
> such a government (at Washington) might be to the in-
> terest of the governed. But there are none such on our
> political horizon and *we cannot expect a complete reversal
> of all of the teachings of history.*
> "To bring about government by oligarchy, masquerading
> as democracy, it is fundamentally necessary that prac-
> tically all authority and control be centralized in our
> national government."

There, in very truth, is the prescription to fascism. Are we
taking it, or are we not?

Many of these idolators of the State (not the states) are, no
doubt, influenced by the highest motives. Others are confused

as they see no alternative. But we are blind indeed if we do not recognize that there are many others in this country who know exactly what they are doing, and why they are doing it,—to seize power *at the throat of government,* whether it be fascism or communism.

Jefferson and his colleagues knew it was not wise to concentrate power at a single place, in a single person. They believed in the distribution of power even at the cost of some efficiency. They did not think it was wise to concentrate all of the pressures for the survival of free government at a single point. They would redistribute the hazards of that survival in the same way that a single insurance company today will not accept an enormous risk. It will take the risk only if it can reinsure it upon a broad base.

The Jeffersonians of today do not wish to place their entire future at the hazard of unpredictable pressures at a single point. Democracy emerged, like Phoenix from its ashes, from all earlier panics in our history because it had not given guarantees that no storms would ever come. When the promissory notes being given today by our government mature and cannot be met, it will be a sad day for democracy.

That is the danger of government undertaking the performance of economic function. It has about all it can do in umpiring the game, without taking part in it. Look at our crime record for example. Justice Brandeis once said—

> "Our government does not yet grapple successfully with the duties it has assumed and should not extend its operations at least until it does."

In the last analysis, whether business is run by business men or by government officials, it is still run by human beings. There are some good men at Washington but no gods. It is a child's illusion that a uniform gives wisdom to the wearer. Business men, actuated by the profit motive may, and too often do, yield to greed for gold. But the greed for power has caused the greater human wreckage. It is the most intoxicating wine man has ever drunk.

"The paths of glory lead but to the grave." It was not the love of money that caused Napoleon to turn Europe into a charnel house. It was his soaring ambition, his desire to place one of his brothers on every throne in Europe. And so, drunk with power, it was possible for him, after the Battle of Bautzen, to write to his Empress

"My health is good. I put my losses at 3,000 killed and wounded. *I lost no one of any importance.*"

CHAPTER 7

MAN OR THE STATE

"It is time to make an effort to reverse that process of the concentration of power which has made most American citizens, once traditionally independent owners of their own businesses, helplessly dependent for their daily bread on the favor of the very few."

—Franklin D. Roosevelt.

We are told today that we have only two choices, Big Business or Big Government. We instinctively revolt against each alternative. We know that each breeds nothing but "yes men"; we know that each involves "absentee landlords"; the bureaucrat at Washington and the "economic royalist" in New York. We know that the political machine collects tribute in the same way that the financial machine collects tribute. Judging from a nine billion dollar budget, we know that the taxes collected by the political machine together with campaign "kick-ins" (if nothing worse) is as great or greater than the tribute wrung by the "money-changers." Careful students of the problem estimate that the spoils system, alone, costs a billion a year.

We know that the "concentration of power" whether in Wall Street or in Washington makes the citizen "helplessly dependent" on the favor of the "very few." We know that in either case the middle class, which contains the largest number of Americans who actually care for democracy, is in danger of being ground to powder between the upper and nether millstones of exactions wrung by monopoly on the one hand, and taxes to subsidize pressure groups on the other.

And yet, knowing these things to be true, we follow the law

of the pendulum. We swing from the abuses of "private social-ism" to the dangers of "Federal socialism."

Are these the only two choices left us? Is there not a middle ground between these extremes?

In approaching this subject we should ask one question only —"What form of government will produce the greatest good for the greatest number?" It is not our obligation to worship our ancestors nor cling to theories which have had the sanction of great names—just because these men were great. Their great-ness, which has survived the attrition of time, may indeed give the principles they believed in the presumption of being sound. Men become great only because of the greatness of their beliefs or their actions. Nevertheless Jefferson was entirely right when he said, "The earth belongs to the living." If any part of our institutions no longer serves the "greatest good of the greatest number," put it in the attic. I am entirely willing to rest the argument wholly upon the question whether these latter mani-festations of the Second or Third New Deal will actually pro-mote the happiness of this generation and the next. Let it stand or fall on that one point.

The trend today is away from liberty and toward what is called "security." But when you have turned the pyramid of government to rest on the apex of one-man or one-party rule, how secure is it? And what is the price for even its *promise* of security?

Part of the price will be the gradual and finally complete loss of all civil rights as government, either by deliberate choice or from the force of circumstance, takes over the responsibility for the economic welfare of all its citizens. As it makes deeper and deeper commitments for their economic welfare, and issues more and more promises for their prosperity, it is perfectly plain that government will increasingly become less tolerant of any and all opposition which may develop with reference to the means it chooses to redeem its promises. Government and public officials are then "on the spot."

We have seen this in America in the past few years. In agriculture we started off with a program which was offered to the farmer as being a matter of voluntary choice. From that, however, we went to the Potato Law which threatened to fine and imprison anybody who did not accept the government's program. As the government, and the political party in control of government, is called upon to produce the "promised land" it will tolerate criticism less and less. This means a gradual diminution of freedom of the press, freedom of assembly, freedom to speak, and the right to teach, to learn, and even to think; and as these rights go, one by one, the right to vote your opposition and criticism will go also. Such has been the course in other lands, now and throughout all history.

And as the right to criticise and to oppose is gradually curtailed, then the right and power of the people to correct abuses is curtailed also. And so the old tyrannies return, and except for a resort to arms, the people are without remedy.

Across the Atlantic the Torch of Liberty has gone out in three-fourths of Europe. The swing toward one-man government daily gathers momentum. New barbarians march on ancient Romes, and place Caesar's blood-rusted crown on the fevered heads of those who call themselves the "saviors of the people." The destruction of civil rights goes hand in hand with this development. Within a short distance of the place where the Prisoner of Chillon once appealed "from tyranny to God," machine guns and concentration camps do the debating when political arguments arise. And while the German blood purge of June 1934 was on, a new messiah shouted, "During these 24 hours I am the Supreme Court."

Democracy is proclaimed a "rotten corpse"; liberalism is spat upon; the authority of religion is spurned; the sanctity of private contract and public treaty is held for naught; the temple of international law, painfully built during five centuries of time, is overthrown, and all those immemorial decencies between man and the state,—trial by jury, the independence of the courts, habeas corpus, the civil above the military power, freedom of petition, of election, of speech, of assembly, of worship, of marriage, of the education of one's children, government by law and not by men, government which derives its "just powers" from the "consent of the governed," the restraint against spoliation and confiscation, the assurance that if a man sow he may also reap (the one driving force other than the lash of the slave which makes wealth to accumulate and the arts and sciences to flourish)—all these precious things are tossed into the sewer as the synthetic parade follows the modern Imperator who rattles his crimsoned sword and scans dark horizons for more worlds to conquer.

Here in America worshippers of the State (not the "states") grow in number. Bearing a banner with that strange device "special privileges for all" they come to Washington seeking alms. Members of church, labor, youth, and women's organizations are sponsoring the surrender of human destiny to politicians idealized as demigods.

Big Government is a poor alternative to Big Business. In fact, if the only alternative to economic autocracy were a political autocracy, I would prefer the former. I might be a wage slave, but as long as my government is free, and my newspaper is free, and the ballot box is open, and my vote is counted, and the judge on the bench is beyond control, I can fight for my freedom and struggle against my fate.

But under a political autocracy, all weapons of defense are taken away. Economic destiny is dictated by government, and protests are answered with guns. When government becomes guardian, the very necessity to make its program succeed means the end of civil rights. What are civil rights? *They are rights against government.*

Even religion, which is based upon the dignity of man as a child of God, is considered, and rightly so, the enemy of the authoritarian state. And how far back towards the Middle Ages has mankind gone in this matter? Mussolini, for example, says that Italians must be Fascists, that is, party members, before they are Catholics. In Germany the Hohenzollern said, "Me and God"; Hitler says "Me or God." They call this progress!

One of the most dangerous elements involved in teaching people to look to government for salvation is that government will be held responsible for its promises. If, which God forbid, there be another crash like 1929, it will be Washington, D. C., and not Wall Street, that will get the blame.

"Economic royalists" will be glad that the blame has been shifted from them, but it will be a sad day for democracy. Then, as always, the old excuse will be made, that the failure was due to insufficient power, and a new crisis psychology will call for the Strong Man himself, who thrice declining the crown at last permits duty to overcome his modesty! Such is the pathology of republics.

Democracy is the finest, but it is the most difficult, of all governments. It gives the most but it takes the most. And one of the deep questions of today is whether we are worthy of it.

Many who want to believe in democracy have lost heart. The long depression, the suffering of the people, the indifference of the masses, the refusal to vote, the unwillingness of the ablest citizens to hold public office or to sit on juries, the corruption of political machines, the purchase of votes from the public treasury, the appeal to prejudice and ignorance, the demagogue with his power multiplied a millionfold by the radio and the silver screen, the helplessness of the very poor who have no real choice except to hope that the siren in politics really knows, the universal preoccupation in the tasks of daily living, the movement of the people away from the sun and the soil to the city, the increase in tenancy, the dilution of the bloodstream of those who have the "feel" of Plymouth Rock, the loss of the American frontier, the psychological shock of the World War, the cruel injustices of the business cycle, technological unemployment displacing vast numbers of willing workers, the average age line moving up as child and adult mortality is conquered, the industrial deadline constantly moving down to lower age levels, thus shutting off the most priceless of all gifts—opportunity; the lengthening years since Washington and Franklin, and Jefferson and Lincoln; the loss of "constitutional morality"; the weakening of the authority of parents, pastors, priests, the sense of distance between governor and governed, the hopeless feeling that one does not count . . . !

Such is the catalogue of difficulties confronting democracy. No wonder it has raised up powerful critics. No wonder it has put our capacity for self-government under greater strain than we have ever known. No wonder that it challenges constitutional democracy and free enterprise. And so we see across the Atlantic, and on this side of the Atlantic, those who sneer at the institutions of our fathers which, they say, worked well in the "horse and buggy days," but are wholly unfitted for the twentieth century.

We find ourselves, therefore, between those ready and anxious to scrap democracy, on the one hand, and on the other, faint hearts unwilling to defend it.

Shall we "call it a day" and quit? Have we become so soft that we are no longer willing to fight, as our fathers did, for democracy? If so we shall have sinned beyond absolution. The fault will not be in our leaders, whether statesmen or rabble-rousers. It will be in us.

Confronted with questions like these, there is a tonic effect in a page of history. Robert E. Lee once wrote—

"The truth is this: The March of Providence is so slow and our desires so impatient; the work of progress is so immense and our means of aiding it so feeble; the life of humanity is so long and that of the individual so brief, that we often see only the ebb of the *advancing* wave and are discouraged. It is history that teaches us to hope."

Yes, history teaches us to hope. The difficulties confronting us today, however different, are certainly not greater than those which confronted Jefferson and Washington and Lincoln. The same indifference, the same plots and counterplots, the same arguments, the same cabals, the same babel of voices, the same summer soldiers and sunshine patriots, the same distrust of democracy. The difference between ourselves and our fathers is that they had nothing but hope. They had nothing but an unwritten page. We have the record of 150 years.

"A little patience and we shall see the reign of witches over, their spells dissolve and the people, recovering their true sight restore their government to its true principles."

Such was Jefferson's confidence in the common sense of his generation. We have seen one hundred and thirty million people meet the heartaches of the last eight years. We have seen homes, farms, savings, jobs swept away. With what undaunted courage, with what essential integrity of the human spirit, with what self-control, did our people watch that flood. It is, in fact, one of the greatest chapters not only in our history, but in the annals of mankind.

The heart of our people is still sound! That has been demonstrated by their performance of the last eight years.

Our problem is not new except in its application. Fisher Ames, one of the great orators of the Revolutionary period, thought it all out 150 years ago—

"If all you want is a smooth running machine, an absolute monarchy is the best the world has ever devised. A monarchy is like a man of war, beautiful in motion, irresistible when under way, but a single hidden rock sends her to the bottom; while democracy is like a raft, always in trouble, your feet always wet, but nothing can sink her."

The problem was correctly stated by President Roosevelt at the beginning of this chapter—"to reverse the process of concentration of power." But he has sought concentration of political power to offset concentration of economic power. At the last, the two things become one, as Fascism proves.

Mr. Roosevelt seems to have become fainthearted with democratic processes back in the counties, cities, states. Especially since the 1936 election he has sought remedies only in Washington. He seems, unfortunately, to have lost faith in the essential principle of Jefferson; to decentralize government and thereby revitalize democracy.

CHAPTER 8

EXHIBIT A—WASHINGTON, D. C.

Before proceeding further to obliterate the states, counties, cities, and towns; before wiping out the last trace of local responsibility of cities and citizens and turning over to the Great White Father at Washington the welfare of 130 million people, let us see how Washington, D. C., is run. Let us take a look at the demi-gods of Federalism behind the scene.

As Exhibit A of the blessings of centralized government, all-wise and all-powerful, in which our people have such a childlike faith, Washington, D. C., is an excellent case study. This is so, among other things, because we can refer to it without raising any partisan or political question. While some new buildings have gone up in Washington during the present administration, the picture which this chapter will present, is wholly impartial as between Democratic or Republican administrations. Both parties have been in charge at Washington; the Republican party, in fact, for the longer period. As a result the question of credit or blame for efficiency, or the lack of it, ceases to be a party issue.

The government at Washington goes on year after year, decade after decade, whatever party is in power. Washington is the capital of the nation. It is located in the District of Columbia. This district is exclusively Federal territory and has been such since the capital was moved to Washington, 138 years ago. During that long period of time responsibility for things in the nation's capital has been entirely and exclusively a responsibility of the Federal government, to whom we are now asked to surrender our destinies.

48

Washington, D. C., is not a "blighted area" or "abandoned stepchild" of the states. Its present condition does not come from their neglect because they have not "the heavenly vision." Nor is it the discard of cruel and selfish "interests" who exploit our timberlands, our coal deposits, our copper mines, and having thus exploited them move on to other areas, thoughtless of what they leave in their wake. Whatever Washington is, it is the sole responsibility of our *national* government.

Washington is a city of magnificent distances. It is rapidly becoming one of the most beautiful capitals in the world. It has many imposing public buildings, the sight of which gives pride to the visiting American. I believe a great nation like ours should take pride in its capital city. I think one should get a lift of inspiration when one sees for the first time the home of the national government. I think that, within reason, we should tax ourselves to have a capital in which we can take pride.

Having said this, it must yet be said that the beauty of Washington comes only from taxes poured in by the people back home. The wealth represented by these lovely buildings is not produced in Washington. What is spent there is that much less available to be spent back in the states and the cities and the homes of our citizens. Many a home in America might be resplendent in a new coat of paint except for the fact that the home-owner, after paying taxes to support his Federal government, did not have enough left to buy his paint.

Having said this, let us take a closer look at Washington, the capital of the nation, the baby of Uncle Sam. Let us go through this experiment station of Federal government. Let us see how Uncle Sam has raised his own baby. It will be worth our while to do so before we turn our own babies over to his tender care; before we abandon state rights to his protection.

Every community is first of all interested in its own health. That is one of the things that our Chambers of Commerce brag about with respect to their own localities. How about

Washington and the health of the people who live in our Federal city? For the year 1936, per 100,000 population, the vital statistics of Washington and the nation show that the death rate in the District of Columbia was 26% higher from cancer than the same death rate in the whole United States; 27% higher from heart disease; 49% higher and going up from pneumonia; 92% higher from tuberculosis; 106% higher from alcoholism; 119% higher from syphilis. So, on this vital question of health, put down the home of the Federal government on one side and on the other side the average of health conditions throughout the rest of the nation. Then ask yourself whether the Federal government is doing such a good job in comparison with what is being done back in your home town, as to lead you to want it to take complete responsibility for the health of your own children.

For every 1000 live births in the District of Columbia, the infant mortality rate is 26% higher than that of the whole United States, and the maternal death rate is 91% higher. Perhaps I should again remind you that I am giving figures about Washington, D. C., not one of the abandoned coal towns of West Virginia or a mill town in the South. These are the figures of the model city of a benevolent paternalism.

I should further remind you that it is the home of the Bureau of Public Health Service of the mightiest nation in the world. It is where the health officers of the Federal government themselves live.

And what about crime? That is a subject that interests people in the town where they might settle and raise their children. Washington is not without police officers. It is not that trustful of humanity. In fact, Washington has five separate police forces, the Metropolitan or City Police, the Capitol Police, the White House Police, the Park Police, and the Zoo Police. It is also the home of the G-men, "masters of crime." It is where they live and breathe and have their being. It is the city of the Department of Justice of the Federal government.

It is the one city and the one district in which the Federal government has sole and exclusive authority and jurisdiction on all matters of law and order.

How does Washington compare in this important matter of crime with other cities in the United States? The comparison has been made by the chief law officer of the Federal government, Honorable Homer S. Cummings, Attorney General of the United States. This is what Mr. Cummings said last January at a meeting of the Washington Crime Forum:

"The crime situation in the District of Columbia *amounts to a national disgrace*. Washington should be a model city.

"Authentic statistics, covering the period from July to September, 1937, inclusive, indicate that out of *ninety-three cities with a population of more than* 100,000, Washington ranks in the *10 per cent. of cities* with the *most crime* and that Washington is the *tenth* from the top of a list in the number of *murders* and *non-negligent manslaughters*. In the number of aggravated assaults it is *eighth* from the top of the list. In the number of automobile thefts it is *seventh*. In the number of *thefts* under $50. it is *sixth*. In the number of thefts more than $50. it is *third*. In the number of *robberies* it is *seventh*. In the number of burglaries and housebreakings it is *fifth*.

"Our resourcefulness as a city and as a nation is at a low level if we can't control major crimes and racketeering in an area of seventy square miles. The District of Columbia should be a model for the country—clean and free from lawlessness. Instead it *stands forth conspicuously as a crime center*."

This is not Chicago, Ill., or St. Louis, Mo., or New Orleans, La. This is Washington, D. C. It is an example of how the Federal government does things. It is what we find on the other side of the magnificent public buildings.

The next thing which the average citizen and his wife are interested in is housing. Let us look beyond these "magnificent distances" in Washington and see what exists in the nation's capital. The real property inventory of 1934, taken under the auspices of the United States, shows that in its capital city, there were more than 14,000 dwelling units without inside toilets; more than 4000 without inside running water; more than 11,000 using kerosene lamps, more than 6000 needing major repairs; more than 2000 dwelling units unfit for use. Only two of the 64 American cities surveyed in this real property inventory had more houses unfit for use, or in need of major repairs but in use.

This is not some city whose people dwell in regimented shacks built by soulless corporations. We are not writing of conditions in Harlan County, Ky., where the Federal government charges that the coal barons condemn their wage slaves to wretchedness. This, I must again remind you, as it is necessary for me to constantly remind myself, is Uncle Sam's home. There is no large industry in Washington, no factories, no coal mines, no denuded hillsides. This is Washington. It is the place where the Federal Housing Administration lives and where the Home Owners Loan Corporation has offices aircooled by the taxpayers living back home.

Washington, D. C., is also a city as little affected by the peaks and valleys of the economic cycle as any city in America. No factories close their doors on willing workers in Washington. The tentacles of the robber barons of Wall Street do not here condemn the citizens of Washington to the conditions I have detailed. It is a city of steady employment, of men and women paid from the longest purse in the world. As recently computed, it is the home of 111,130 Federal employees, and constantly growing in number, who never knew there was a depression in America in the years following 1929 until in March 1933 when they were asked to take a 15% pay cut. The plight of thousands in private industry taking a 50% or 100% pay cut and being without jobs for months and years on end, is not responsible for conditions at Washington, the model city of a benevolent paternalism.

One-third of the nation is ill-housed. We don't have to go down South to find them. It is not necessary to look that far. One need only lean out of a window in the Senate office building and see, and hear, and smell Schotts Alley, notorious for crime and disease.

Well, how about education? There is something that interests the fathers and mothers of America,—education in the nation's capital. In October 1937, there were four school buildings housing 1537 pupils, which buildings had been recommended for early abandonment in 1908—*29 years ago, but were still in use*.

In other school buildings classes were being held in basement rooms, play rooms, and corridors. A shift system was in effect in some schools in the nation's capital wherein two sets of children in the lower grades used the same room for shortened class periods. Although the normal class size is 35 to 40 pupils, there were 46 classes in excess of 50 pupils, and some classes ran up to as many as 84 children. There were 2478 grade school children in classes in excess of the normal 40 to a class. There were 3789 Junior and Senior High School students in excess of capacity.

We have heard much recently about the Federal government taking over the education of the children of the nation on the ground that the states and the cities are doing such a lamentable job. The uplifters and the bureaucrats constantly think up new reasons for extending their activities and increasing their payrolls. But in Washington, D. C., in the year of our Lord, 1937, of the many versions of the little red school house, there were 14 one-room grade schools, set up in play ground space, and heated by a coal stove in the rear of the room.

I should add at this point that Washington, D. C., is the home of the Office of Education, housed in the magnificent building of the Department of the Interior, which is constantly engaged in advising the rest of the nation how to educate its children.

At this point it may be of some interest to quote from the Report of the Advisory Committee on Education, appointed by President Roosevelt, in its report of February 1938; they say—

> "The Committee has detailed the situation of the District of Columbia at some length, because it believes that in no instance of Federal relationships to local conduct of education has the Federal government departed so far from the spirit of American institutions. . . . The Committee thinks that in recommending Federal aid for education throughout the United States it would indeed be delinquent if it did not recommend first of all that the Federal government set its own house in order."

I have no desire to be unjust to the agencies of the Federal government responsible for governing the city of Washington. Many of them are as devoted to the public service as any which can be found in the United States. I have no desire to be unjust to the citizens of Washington. They are as anxious that their city rank at the top with reference to housing, health, education, crime, and these other matters which enter so intimately into the happiness of the American home, as the people living anywhere. And Washington has problems of its own. But these problems, although they may be different, are probably no more difficult than the problems which public officials have to wrestle with in the average American city.

These Federal officials at Washington will say, and perhaps with entire propriety, that they do not have sufficient funds, that they are handicapped in their work. This may be so but when they say, "Give us more money and we will clean up Washington," it is only fair to ask "Where will the money come from?" The more spent in Washington of Federal tax money, the less money is available to be spent back in Milwaukee, and Dayton, and Springfield, and South Bend. The more money that is taken from these cities to improve conditions at Washington makes it more difficult for them to carry on back home.

The same dollar cannot be spent twice for the same thing. As a matter of fact, the chapter "Starving the States" shows that the enormous sums now being spent by the Federal government is making it less possible for the towns and cities outside of Washington to deal with their own problems of crime, health, housing, schools, and the like.

My only purpose in presenting the seamy side of Washington is to disillusion the millions of our people who believe that the Federal government is better than state and local governments; that the badge worn by the bureaucrat of Washington makes him wiser, less selfish, more far-visioned than the public officials whom you elect back home to run the affairs of your own community.

This record of Washington is a Stop, Look and Listen sign to everyone who is tempted to abandon state rights, home rule, and local responsibility for the doubtful blessings of Federalism.

When you are requested by Federal officials, whose salaries are paid by taxes taken from your own pocket, to hand over your destinies to them, it would be well to reflect upon the parable of the man in olden times who was advised to remove the beam in his own eye before he undertook to remove the mote from the eye of his neighbor.

CHAPTER 9

THE DYING KING

"Were we to be directed from Washington when to sow and when to reap, we should soon want bread."

"Our country is too large to have all of its affairs directed by a single government."

—Jefferson.

"While the Brazilian government was paying men to grow coffee to be burned and the United States government was paying farmers not to grow cotton, the Sao Paulo government was spending funds to recruit labor in Europe to grow cotton in Brazil. Such coincidences do not tend to increase one's confidence in government planning and supervision as a means of correcting the existing maladjustments in the economic world."

—Melvin T. Copeland.

Let us turn from the misgovernment of Washington, the Federal city, to the equally unsatisfactory results of planning on the grand scale.

Let us consider the case of the dying king—Cotton.

Some 10% of the American people depend for their livelihood on cotton, its growth, ginning, transportation, and processing. That is to say, some twelve million people. Cotton is the chief source of wealth in many important states. In recent years, westward the course of its empire has taken way to Oklahoma, West Texas, Arizona and Southern California. It is, *or was*, our largest export crop. Our ability to sell our cotton abroad as well as at home has told the story, in large part, of good times or bad for many generations of our people, first in the South, and second throughout the nation.

Again, as in the case of our Capital City, we can be entirely impartial in this matter. Since 1928 both the Republican party and the Democratic party have tried to "save" cotton. With the best intentions in the world; with the longest purse in the world; with the best brains government can induce into its service, two great parties have tried their hand with the problem of cotton. Both have failed. Both have created new problems for every old problem they poulticed.

Again, this is not a question of "objectives." Nor of human sympathy. The sharecropper in the South, black and white, is at the base of the agricultural pyramid. He is a part of the one-third of our nation that is said to be ill-fed, ill-clothed, and ill-housed. No decent citizen can fail to wish his lot improved. Perhaps a way can yet be found. But, from the record, what is the actual accomplishment of ten years of Washington attempting to tell the South when to sow and when to reap? No one can blame the cotton growers of the South, bad as their condition has been, for accepting the different government programs which have been offered them. Their immediate needs made it impossible for them to consider the long range cost of the program.

In 1928 cotton was about 18¢. Under President Hoover the Farm Board was set up. It cost us in the neighborhood of a cool half-billion. Under it, we started to peg prices by loaning money on cotton. We hid cotton away in government warehouses so it would not depress the cotton in the open market. In 1930, we passed the Smoot-Hawley tariff bill which doubled average duties over rates prevailing a decade previously. And, for the sake of the record, let it be said that the first public official of prominence to advise restriction of cotton acreage, which has since become known as the Plow-Up Program, was

Mr. Hyde, former Governor of Missouri and President Hoover's Secretary of Agriculture.

When the New Deal was voted into power in 1933, cotton had gone down from 18¢ in 1928 to 5.5¢. Such was the record of the Republican administration.

In the 1932 campaign we Democrats in our party platform condemned "the unsound policy of restricting agricultural production to the demands of domestic markets." Having won the election on that platform pledge, we proceeded at once to adopt the "unsound policy." We called it by a different name but we did not make it a different thing. Roses, however named, smell the same.

In a campaign speech in Kansas in September 1932, Mr. Roosevelt put it this way—

> "When the futility of maintaining prices of wheat and cotton through so-called stabilization became apparent, the President's Farm Board, of which his Secretary of Agriculture was a member, invented the cruel joke of advising farmers to allow 20% of their wheat lands to lie idle, to plow up every third row of cotton, and to shoot every tenth dairy cow."

Instead of the Farm Board, we Democrats produced the "processing tax." Under it we also pegged prices by loaning money on cotton. We also stored cotton in warehouses so as not to compete with cotton on the free market. And by the tax collected from the consumers of cotton goods, we paid cotton growers not to grow cotton, the "objective" if not the exact method advocated by the Republican Secretary of Agriculture Hyde. The "New Deal" was begotten by the New Era.

We have nearly a decade of experience in the attempt to control cotton from Washington under two administrations of two great political parties. What is the result? I quote Secretary Wallace, in his speech at Memphis, Tennessee, October 1, 1937.

"This year's production of *foreign* cotton will probably be eight or nine million bales more than foreign production five years ago." (1932)

Meantime, on a restricted acreage we produced in 1937 more cotton than ever before in our history. This was due to the perversity of Mother Nature and the very human instinct of Southern cotton farmers to concentrate their efforts and fertilizer on their best acres, as they took the poor acres out of cultivation.

From 1928 to 1932 we averaged 40,554,000 acres planted to cotton. The huge crop of 1938 is being grown on 26,904,000 acres. This means that 13,650,000 acres of tillable land in the South has been taken out of the production of cotton. This is equivalent to *all* the land in Massachusetts, Connecticut, Rhode Island and Delaware, and two additional Delawares, assuming that every acre in these states, even including the land occupied by their cities and highways, had been planted to cotton. Figuratively, it is the same as if a barbed wire fence had been stretched around these states with the warning sign "no cotton allowed."

This has resulted in throwing out of work thousands of farm hands as it takes less manpower to cultivate these millions of acres *less*. I have been advised that there is a secret report in the files of the Department of Agriculture indicating that two million men have been thrown out of work in the South as a result of the acreage curtailment.

Meantime Brazil, Egypt, India, China, Russia and other countries planted millions of acres *more* and again with what result?

In 1931 America furnished 45% of all cotton consumed abroad. In 1936 we furnished 32%. In 1937 23%. Another way of stating it is that in 1911-1913 we grew 64% of the world's production; in 1937, 37% of the total.

In 1936-7 the consumption of our cotton in foreign mills was 2,000,000 bales *less* than in 1933-4, and the consumption of foreign grown cotton 6,000,000 bales *more*. Thus farmers in other lands grew and sold some millions of bales that our farmers were paid *by our consumers* not to produce!

While this was going on, while we were turning over our foreign market to foreign cotton growers, our Export-Import Bank financed the sale of American cotton ginning machinery to Brazil so that as a result of our good neighbor policy, Brazil might not only grow the cotton that we formerly grew but could gin it besides. This goes by the name of "planning"!

If this program continues by progressive steps to the ultimate total destruction of our foreign cotton market, we will then be growing our domestic cotton requirements on 16 or 17 million acres compared with the 40,554,000 acre average, a reduction of some 23 million acres in the South with no satisfactory alternative crop yet developed. Twenty-three million acres is the size of the State of Indiana, assuming that every acre of the Hoosier State had been devoted to the growing of cotton, and were to be taken out of production.

As we have been gradually turning over our foreign customers to foreign growers, a fact of momentous social significance is that for each five bales of cotton so lost to the South, one Southern family, man, wife and children, go on relief of some kind. So as the South loses its revenues from the sale of cotton abroad, Federal relief rolls in the South must be increased.

What is the long range price of this decade of effort at Washington to tell the South when to sow and when to reap? It is the loss, permanently in all probability, of a large part of our world trade in cotton. It may be a generation, perhaps longer, before we recover by finding substitute crops and new markets.

And what will the South do with these millions of newly idle acres and newly idle men? They can do and will do one of three things or a combination of the three; any one or the combination having its adverse effect somewhere else in the nation.

First, the South can grow on these acres taken out of cotton other crops for Southern markets heretofore grown in the North,—corn, potatoes, garden truck, cattle, dairy products, etc. In many ways a diversification of agriculture in the South would benefit it. But it is apparent that as the South grows these other crops, it will by that same token, invade the markets of Northern farmers who heretofore have grown these crops; further increase the problem of farm surpluses in the North, and further depress agricultural commodity prices in the North. In other words, the "planned economy" program has to be paid for by someone, somewhere, sometime, somehow.

In enacting the present A.A.A. law there was a bitter struggle in Congress, especially by the Representatives from the great dairying sections of the North, against permitting land withdrawn from cotton cultivation in the South from being used to produce dairy products, except for the Southern farmer and his immediate family. Nevertheless, we find Southern dairy products entering the Northern market.

Second, the men, black and white, thrown out of work by the cotton curtailment program in the South, can migrate to the industrial labor centers in the North, thus competing with Northern labor as Southern crops are now competing with Northern crops and acting as a deadweight on Northern wage scales and Northern prosperity.

Third, if these idle men are not employed in growing alternative crops in the South or if they do not move into Pittsburgh, Indianapolis, Detroit, Philadelphia, New York, Chicago, etc., what then? They can, and no doubt will as a last desperate alternative, go on the dole permanently to be supported, in part at least, from taxes collected by the Federal government in the North. In short, this unemployed Southern labor must either compete with Northern agriculture, Northern labor, or go permanently on relief.

As Secretary Wallace himself said, it is a problem whether—

"jobs and livelihood could constantly be found in industry for several hundred thousand of these workers no longer needed to grow cotton."

Mr. Wallace is a sincere and honest man, and he himself poses the question whether you can curtail cotton production in the South without the price having to be paid by someone, somewhere, somehow, sometime.

One thing more can be said about the long range effect of a decade of artificial cotton restriction. In 1928 cotton was 18¢. In 1933 it was 5.5¢. From that low it went up to about 13.5¢. In the fall of 1937 it was 7.5¢. And for today's market read the evening newspaper. In terms of the old dollar value given to an ounce of gold, cotton *is now lower than at any time in the history of this country*.

So, after eight years, under two administrations, Republican and Democratic, and after the expenditure of hundreds of millions of dollars, cotton has never been as high as when we started to save it!

So much for cotton. Other crops, wheat, corn, etc., and other sections of the country could have been used instead, but cotton is the most important crop as to which production by statute has been attempted. Space does not permit a discussion of these other efforts by a centralized government, a centralized and no longer Jeffersonian government, to artificially boost prices for our farm products. But a summary is of interest.

"Indices of World Production of Foodstuffs" from the World Economic Survey of the League of Nations, using 1925-29 as 100, show that world production of foodstuffs for the years 1929, 1930, 1932, 1934, 1935 rose to 103, 104, 106, 106, 104. *American production* of foodstuffs for these same years, using the same basis of 1925-29 as 100, fell to 91, 96, 68, 66, 76.

So while we were reducing our production of foodstuffs to two-thirds or three-quarters of the 1925-29 average, the world outside of the United States was producing more than during the base period, and *selling their surplus to us,* as recent import figures have demonstrated. Of course, some of this was due to the severe drouths of recent years.

There has been some apparent immediate benefit from these curtailment programs. But can any one project these programs over a 10, 20, or 30-year period and escape coming to the conclusion that in the long run the nation and *particularly the farmer* will pay a heavy price, with compound interest, for all immediate benefits?

Realizing the depressed economic condition of our agriculture since the World War, I hope there is no decent American anywhere who would not join in saying that if there were some way to *permanently* benefit the cotton belt, or the corn belt, or the wheat belt, or other crop belts, by action of the Federal government, and without doing compensating injury elsewhere, he would rejoice to see it done.

But there are some things bureaucracy is not able to do. There are some things the Federal government, great and powerful as it is, is unable to do. For one thing it cannot police the farmers of the world. Mrs. Partington could not sweep back the sea.

Uncle Sam has been holding an umbrella, supplied by the American taxpayer, over our foreign competitors.

The situation was well described by Senator Walter George of Georgia in a speech in the Senate March 28, 1935, in which he said:

> "What is happening is that Mr. Wallace, under the A.A.A. is paying benefits to the farmers. He is paying us to plow up our cotton and to kill off our hogs and to reduce our acreage and to reduce our production, but how is he doing it? He is doing it by asking the American farmer to sell out his business; to sell out his capital investment. . . . We have sold our farm business for a mess of pottage, for one or two years of benefit favors."

CHAPTER 10

THE FARMER AND FREE ENTERPRISE

Even when times are good, the wise storekeeper watches his credit risks, looks over his insurance policies, and keeps his weather eye peeled for forces that may affect adversely his earnings and his savings. A wise nation will do the same thing. No such permanent and drastic changes have yet been made in our lives and way of living as have been made in some of the nations of Europe. Now is a good time, therefore, to take stock of the ideas and forces loose in the world which may affect profoundly the nature and future of our agriculture.

The world is now divided into two camps. In one camp are those who believe that the future can best be served by a system of free enterprise, with such controls by government as may be likened to those traffic rules which are necessary on crowded streets. In the other camp are those who believe that modern conditions require that the state shall become the supreme dictator of our lives and our enterprises.

Sooner or later all of us must make up our minds about these two camps. The way affairs are moving the world around, there will be no half-way house between the two camps. We shall have to be in one or the other. In which of these camps will the American farmer be most prosperous as a producer and happiest as a citizen? I want, if I can, to strike an honest balance-sheet between these two camps as far as the farmer's interests are involved.

How far should agriculture submit its fate to government, to any government, whether conservative, liberal, or radical? Is there a point *to* which it should go, but *beyond* which it should not go, in the matter of government control and direction? If so, can it stop at that point or will events force it to go the whole hog?

What is the "whole hog" to which events might force it? Recently General Hermann Goering, director of Germany's new economic program, gave us a glimpse of the end of the trail. Stripped of its husks of noble words, the nubbin is this: The German farmer is to become the slave of the state. He will do as he is told, live as he is ordered, earn what is decreed by political authority. Berlin will be his boss.

General Goering has said, as reported by the Agricultural Attaché of our American Embassy in Berlin in 1936, that the goal of the national program is an increase in the gross production of foodstuffs "even if it involves a decrease in net returns" to the farmer. This means compulsion. It must mean compulsion. Men will not, either in Germany, or in America, work harder and longer to produce more and sell it for less unless they are made to.

In March 1937, General Goering issued a decree to the effect that the state will appoint a trustee to run the affairs of any German farmer who fails to meet the demands of the national program. If necessary, he suggested, the state will take absolute control of the land, order the owner to stop farming, and rent the land to another farmer. There are no exceptions. This decree applies to every German farmer.

Three months later, the German government ordered a nation-wide redistribution of agricultural land, pooling large numbers of small farms into large single farming units, with the idea of making each individually operated farm meet the government's standard of efficient production. Roland Freisler, State Secretary of the Ministry of Justice, admits that, under this policy, the ancient fact of land ownership can no longer mean what it has meant to the German farmer for generations. "Every German farmer," he said, "knows now that his relationship to the soil he tills is a working relationship, not merely a matter of title. . . . There is no longer any need or any room for an abstract right of ownership of land."

The program calls for official supervision or even replacement of "incompetent farmers" who fail to meet the state's demand. The goal is increased production at all costs. If the "incompetent" farmer stands in the state's way, neither he nor his farm has any rights the state is bound to respect. The state, in short, applies to the farm what is known as the "stretch out" in industry.

While the state will remove from his farm a farmer who does not please it, the state will not permit farmers to leave farming of their own free will. General Goering has said that the "flight from the land" will be treated as an "evasion of responsibility for the national welfare," or as desertion from the army would be treated. *This means, in blunt words, conscripted farm labor.* It means the draft in peace as well as in war.

A "farm card" system is to be introduced so that the political authorities can have a "detailed picture of the operation and management of every individual farm." The hidden blackjack in this program is plain. Do as you are told. The German industrial worker, by the way, has a similar "card" which amounts to an employer's black list. So many demerits on your "card" and you know your fate.

Perhaps the circumstances of Germany's situation make all this a matter of harsh necessity. I pass no judgment on German policy for German circumstances. But policies and tendencies of this sort are world-wide. You can find them in Russia, in Japan, in Italy, in Mexico. You see them in the Agricultural Crisis Law of 1933 in The Netherlands. We have seen foreshadowings of them in the United States. We remember the compulsory Potato bill, the Tobacco bill, and the Cotton bill of three years ago. These three measures were enacted into law, not in Germany, not in Italy, not in Russia, but in America. They have been repealed. But will they return? Look at the new A.A.A. bill of 1938, and consider where it will end.

It is my earnest hope that we shall meet the very real problems of American agriculture through cooperation rather than compulsion, in freedom rather than serfdom, with the state as servant rather than master.

Leaving out of consideration, for the moment, all thought of the happiness that free men feel just because they are free, leaving out the fact that, throughout all history, wherever and whenever the state has taken complete control of a nation's economic life, it has sooner or later gone on to take equally complete control of the education and religion of the people and of all the instruments through which they have expressed themselves freely, let us look at the cold question of whether compulsion by the state is efficient either for the individual or for the nation. Does compulsion by the state justify itself economically?

Three things limit and, in the end, destroy the efficiency of government when it undertakes to dictate in detail the whole economic life of a people:

First, the men who run governments are not all-wise or infallible. They are, in the main, men of just ordinary ability. A man is no wiser and his motives no purer after he puts on an official badge than before. And a Federal badge instils no greater virtue than a state or county badge. They make mistakes. And when a mistake or miscalculation is made at Rome, Berlin, or Washington, involving a whole people or a whole group of a people, how many more suffer than if the same mistake were made by the same man running his own farm or store!

Second, it is difficult for government officials to make their decisions on the merits and facts alone. Economic questions are likely to get political answers. If one expects a politically appointed Federal Reserve Board, let us say, or any other board under any administration—Republican or Democratic or Fascist or Communist—to clamp down on an expanding and dangerous business boom or enact a necessary tax program preceding or during a political campaign, he should have his head examined. Economic questions, I repeat, are likely to get political answers. And, in the battle of groups at Washington, the group that happens to swing the greatest voting power at the moment is likely to dictate the answer. Witness the fate of agriculture for a half century as it was ground between high tariffs for purchases and free markets for sales when the manufacturer was "in the saddle" at Washington.

Third, when government is boss, fear falls like a blanket over the people. No one dares do anything he thinks a bureaucrat might frown upon. The brains of Russia are today going into retirement because of fear. Everybody waits for orders from above. No one ventures along new lines. With the dead hand of bureaucracy the Revolution is strangling its own children. If in the factory a machine or assemby line breaks down, the foreman knows that he may be charged with deliberate sabotage, with Siberia or the firing squad as the penalty. After a Russian train wreck, it is hard to tell whether more get killed in the wreck or after it. Some time ago, before the recent blood purges, thirty-five employees of the Commissariat for Agriculture, many of them experts in foods, were shot without trial. Their blunder was that they failed to guess right. Under such conditions, the worker takes no chances. He plays safe. He makes no experiments. Engineers and inventors and executives refuse to go ahead until plans are approved by the "party" secretary, who probably knows little or nothing about the plan he approves. It is a grim game of passing the buck—to Moscow. The result is industrial chaos.

Free enterprise has not always distributed fairly the plenty it has created, but the totalitarian state, the state that pulls everything in to the center and runs the whole economic life of the nation with an iron hand, has created no plenty to distribute. In terms of the purchasing power of a day's wages of butter, sausage, beef, or sugar, the workers of Russia, of Germany, and of Italy, where government rules the roost, receive but a fraction as much as the employed American worker received in the worst years of our depression.

If the whole history of the human race means anything, nations become prosperous as a result of being free.

Nothing such as I have described has taken place in America. And pray God that it never will! But we are talking of ideas and trends that are in the air the world around. We know that these influences are at work. Both Fascist-minded and Communist-minded forces are boring from within, especially in our great industrial centers. We hear of more "plans" for more "controls" of more parts of our economic life. We hear of plans for the political "allocation of credit" between capital investment and consumer goods. No new industry, we are told, is to get credit if it proposes to enter the field of an established industry which government considers "overbuilt." May not an "overbuilt" industry be one which has political influence and is capable of contributing to the party war chest?

Who is wise enough to decide all these things? Suppose such a system had been in operation when many of the things that now make life livable were struggling to be born. Suppose the phonograph or piano industry, strongly entrenched in Washington, had been able to convince the government that the industry was "overbuilt" and that the infant radio industry should be throttled. Suppose the wagon and street car had, in like manner, stopped the development of the automobile; that natural ice had blocked the refrigerator; that the musician's union had strangled the movietone; that whale oil had prevented kerosene; that natural gas had denied electricity the right to develop. All these are the result of the daring of free enterprise. None are the brain children of bureaucrats. Free men have moved on in search of most and best for least.

What does all this mean for agriculture?

Whatever may be the whole list of factors involved, the immediate cause of agriculture's difficulty has been the loss of markets. There can hardly be dispute of the facts that the loss of foreign markets, at least, has been due in large part to unwise governmental policies—tariffs, war, drastic restriction of immigration, and the like, over a good stretch of time. At any rate, if the disease is lost markets, the cure is new markets, and the long range solution of our difficulties is finding these new markets for farm commodities, not restriction of our production.

Let the chemist search for new markets in his test tube, and the engineer in his laboratory. Let them be free to dream, to make mistakes without reprisals, to fail, and to succeed. If they can find someone to finance their discoveries or inventions, let no bureaucrat deny them their chance. Let them profit if they succeed. I say this because the future farm is destined, if we keep the track clear, to be a source of raw materials for industry as well as a supplier of food. A hundred pounds of cotton go into every automobile and its tires. Cotton is also used in building cement roads. Goldenrod and milkweed may supplant Brazil as a source of rubber. Slash pine as a source of cellulose and tung oil trees may cover the eroded lands of the South. Paints are being grown on the farm, also paper, synthetic lumber, fiber board, drainage pipes, dyes, perfumes, solvents, resin. Perhaps the greatest possibility is cheap industrial alcohol from vegetable wastes, sawdust, and so on, as a substitute for internal combustion fuels. That secret is still locked in the brain of the inventor and developer, but, if released, it will put millions of unproductive acres to work. The potential industrial markets for farm products are as limitless as the desires and genius of man.

These new markets must be found. Only free men are apt to find them, to finance them, to take the chance of "losing their shirts" or "making their pile" in the development. Laboratories can do more than legislatures. If government were to spend the annual price of one battleship in aiding research for new uses for farm commodities, Thanksgiving Day might mean more when it rolls around.

I do not wish to be misunderstood. There is a legitimate field for government cooperation with agriculture. Some government "controls" may well be necessary. But in the long run, decade after decade, aside from correcting the lack of balance between agriculture and industry caused by manufacturers' tariffs, I am convinced that reasonable interest rates for farm financing, a drastic reduction of the cost of government, lower taxes, and the discovery and development of new markets for farm products will do more for the American farmer than the politicians will ever do.

There is danger in government attempting too much. It may issue promises and encourage hopes that cannot be fulfilled. If faith in government is thus destroyed by events beyond the control of even the best-intentioned public officials, what then?

The great enemy of civilization is Monopoly, whether industrial, financial, or political. Big Government is no more lovely than Big Business. In essence, they are the same.

Let's not put all our eggs or all our liberties in one basket. If we do, our children may have neither liberty nor eggs.

CHAPTER II

STARVING THE STATES

"The power to tax is the power to destroy."
—John Marshall.

The trespass upon States' Rights is not of recent origin. It has been going on for a long time due in part to the sheer laziness of state and local officials, due also to their desire to get "something for nothing," by exchanging their sovereignty for Federal cash.

The more recent developments of this Hamiltonian trend, however, go beyond theory, go beyond abstract conceptions of government however important. Under the Roosevelt administration of the national government this movement toward centralization has gathered momentum until it has become an actual and imminent threat to the very existence of the states, their local governments and their citizens. And this more recent trend has not been due by any means to the passing of the buck, the shifting of responsibility from state and local officials to the wearers of official badges. It has been due to aggressive Federal invasion into state and local government—even against the will of state governors and local officials. The steamroller of Federalism today is crushing out the capacity of states, and their local sub-divisions of government, to carry on their responsibilities.

Most people find difficulty in becoming alarmed over "State Rights." When they think of these problems, however, in terms of their own rights as individual men and women, it becomes another matter, for example, such things as fire, police, water, sewage, libraries, schools, parks, playgrounds. The Federal government today is making it difficult, and unless the trend is reversed, will soon make it impossible for John Citizen and his wife to carry on these important functions of local and state government for their benefit and under *their* control. I refer to the fact that the Federal government is invading and drying up sources of tax revenue back home, by which these governmental functions are carried on.

My authority is Governor Herbert Lehman of New York, who as Chief Executive of that state has the responsibility of some 13 million people with respect to these functions of government so important in the home of every citizen. Governor Lehman has just announced that he has paid off a *deficit* of *ninety-four million dollars* which he inherited from his predecessor, Governor Roosevelt.

The State of New York, by constitutional provision, forbids an operating deficit to be funded, even though the people by majority vote favor covering a deficit with a bond issue. Under its constitution, operating deficits must be charged against the revenues of the succeeding years.

While Governor Lehman has been wrestling with the deficit left him by his predecessor, Governor Roosevelt, Mr. Roosevelt has gone from Albany to Washington and has been creating new and far greater Federal deficits for future presidents to wrestle with.

In addition to the deficit that the Federal government is now incurring, to be paid off by future taxation taken from the earnings of our children, it has been increasing its taxes on the present generation. This has created a threat against the ability of states, such as New York, and their local subdivisions, to carry on their own functions. The problem so created has not been better stated than by Governor Lehman himself in an address at Atlantic City, September 14, 1937, before the Conference of Governors of American States; and later in a letter by him to Senator Pat Harrison, Chairman of the Senate

Finance Committee under date of March 18, 1938. I quote from these statements of Governor Lehman as follows:

"In New York, we have released the general property tax for the exclusive use of the municipalities. The state undertakes to finance its activities by obtaining revenue from other sources. Of the ten important taxes upon which my State depended last year for 84% of its revenue, with but two exceptions the Federal government lays heavy taxes on the same sources. The first in importance is the personal income tax. Our State rates are not high, but federal rates are graduated to as high as 79%. Our maximum corporation tax rate is 6%. The Federal government's top rate is 15%, with an additional tax on undistributed net income, running as high as 27%. Our estate tax is *graduated to 20%*, on the largest estates, while the *federal rates run to 70%*, with a credit against the federal tax of 16%, if paid to a state.

"The right of the states to tax their residents on personal incomes, their authority to tax corporations, their power to lay taxes on the estates of decedents, rests upon as solid a foundation, and in some instances, a more solid one, in logic, morals and law, than does the right, the authority, or the power of the Federal government.

"Assuming, for instance, that any American state should decide to tax personal incomes as high as the Federal government taxes them, what would be the result? The answer is simple. The combined taxes would be unbearably high. They would discourage individual initiative and adversely affect the economy of the nation. Moreover, a taxpayer having an income of $250,000, would find his tax bill $256,500—$6500 more than his income. A similar situation would occur if the states taxed the estates of decedents as high as the Federal government. You will say such a situation is extremely unlikely. To that I agree. But when I tell you that *in two states, the combined federal and state rate is 94% of all income above a certain amount* and in another, 90% above $12,000—you will see the situation is serious. And similar conditions prevail in the taxation of estates. . . .

"Before it is too late, we should consider the effects and consequences of conflicting taxation. Of primary importance is the effect on our national economy. The money needed to pay the aggregate cost of federal, state and local government, should be raised in such fashion as to secure a reasonable distribution of the load and avoid discouraging the development or enlargement of business enterprises. Unless this is done, the economic interests of the nation suffer as well as the interests of the groups directly affected. The assets of a nation consist of its material wealth, natural resources and, as well, the creative, constructive, inventive genius of its people. If two governments with concurrent jurisdiction, lay taxes so high in the aggregate as to discourage the individual, his ability (and he might have added his capital) is withdrawn from the business field and the country loses a valuable asset.

"Other possible consequences may attack the very integrity of the nation. Think, if you will, what would result if the states asserted their rights to tax—say, personal incomes and estates as high as does the Federal government. As we have seen, in incomes and estates of certain size, more than 100% would be consumed in paying the two taxes. Obviously, one or the other would have to give way. Assuming, as probably would be the case, that the supreme government—the national government—prevailed, the laws enacted by the states would be suspended. Concededly, the states might be deprived of the means of financing themselves and their localities. They would become vassal states and their importance as units of government would disappear. I make these statements to bring out sharply possibilities not too difficult to conceive."

In his letter to Senator Harrison, Governor Lehman protested against proposals in the Federal taxation bill with reference to taxes against decedents' estates and gift taxes, without allowing to the decedent's estate a reasonable credit for inheritance taxes levied by the state. As Governor Lehman clearly pointed out, this tendency of the Federal government to absorb the bulk of a large estate deprives the state, in which the decedent was a resident, from taxing the estate and thus makes it increasingly difficult for the state to obtain revenues to carry on state and local functions of government. It is like an outsider laying pipes into your reservoir and draining it.

It is perfectly plain, for example, that if the Federal government taxes an estate up to 70% of its value, that there is only 30% left for the state, of which the decedent was a resident, to tax if the entire estate were taken for taxation, leaving nothing to the heirs. As a matter of fact when the Federal government goes as high as 70% in its taxes, without allowing a reasonable credit for inheritance taxes levied by a state, the state government is practically precluded from levying any tax upon the estate; for the reason that when taxes approach 100% of total value it creates what Governor Lehman calls an "uneconomic" result. For example, it drives the taxpayer to seek residence in some other state or in a foreign country and also discourages the taxpayer from taking business ventures.

"The independent sovereignty of the states is threatened by Federal taxing policies. This country was organized on the theory, and has grown and prospered under a system of independent sovereign states, with exclusive authority in many fields and with independent taxing power—a power not second to but on a parity with the Federal government itself. Under such conditions, if one of two governments having equal, concurrent jurisdiction to levy a tax, actually monopolizes the field to the exclusion or the near exclusion of the other, it may follow that that other government will be destroyed or at least starved into impotency. The extent to which the Federal government has been and is ignoring the rights of the states in the income (personal and corporate) and estate tax fields and virtually monopolizing those fields to the exclusion of the states, is truly alarming. The result is that the bulk of state and local revenue is shouldered on real property and that many of the states and their localities have been forced to enact tax laws not suited to state and local use and *uneconomic* in their effects. I give you these thoughts because I am profoundly convinced of their importance if this country is to continue according to the pattern originally planned."

"The Federal tax fixes a ceiling for state taxes. The proposed federal estate tax is graduated to 70 per cent, and in the case of the larger estates takes considerably more than one-half. In the lower brackets, the percentage taken is as high, if not higher, than should reasonably be exacted. It is unthinkable that the states will superimpose upon the Federal tax still higher duties. Hence, for every practical purpose the rates of state estate taxes will be limited to one-sixth of the Federal rates in the various brackets.

"The proposed law assumes the states have but a one-sixth right to tax estates. . . . Stated bluntly, this ignores the equal rights of the states to levy death duties and for every practical purpose tells these sovereign states that they have a right to but one-sixth of the revenues to be derived from estate taxation. There is no justification for such an attitude on the part of the parent government. Its position cannot be defended. As the states have equal, if not a superior claim to revenue from estate taxation, the credit for death duties should not be less than fifty per cent." . . .

"In closing may I not leave with you two further thoughts which have a bearing on this subject:

"The first is that the states have to plan not only for their own financing but for state aid to their municipal and political subdivisions. Except during war times, the services which the states and their localities render to their people are just as important and beneficial as those rendered by the Federal government. Certainly, they are more intimate and personal. The states are encountering increasing difficulty in devising revenue means for their own financing and the financing of the localities.

"The second is the ultimate effect of existing high rates of taxation on incomes and estates on revenue yields in future years. The yield of these taxes depend in a large measure on the high rates in the middle and higher brackets. The effect of existing estate tax rates and those proposed in the measure before you will be to break up sizeable estates and require the payment of taxes out of capital. . . ."

Governor Lehman has put his finger on a problem that is going to be of increasing importance to every governor, every town official, every mayor, and every citizen of every state. Some day our people are going to come *sharply up against the fact that somebody has to pay the bill* to cover the vast expenditures that are now being made by the Federal government.

It is, of course, perfectly obvious that every dollar the Federal government gets must come out of the pocketbook of some citizen, or business company, resident in some state. The same dollar cannot be used twice for the same purpose. When Uncle Sam takes it from the citizen, then it is no longer available to him to support state and local government. When the Federal government taxes a rich man's estate up to 70% of its value, in the high brackets, that source of tax revenue to the state is, to that extent, exhausted.

It is perfectly clear therefore that the more the Federal government, through its huge expenditures, dries up the streams of wealth created back in the states through the energy of their citizens, the possibility of continuing to carry on state and local government is, as Governor Lehman says "seriously challenged." As he says—"When I tell you that in two states the combined federal and the state rate is 94% of all income above a certain amount and in another, 90% above $12,000—you will see the situation is serious."

In the latter instance it means that for every thousand dollars which a taxpayer makes over $12,000 he is permitted by government to keep only $100—giving the other $900 to government. He pays ninety cents for the privilege of earning a dime. The incentive of the citizen to further risk his health and his capital in the expansion of his business,—where if he fails, he takes the entire loss and if he succeeds the government only leaves him 10% of his winnings,—is something for our people to think about as they look hopefully to new enterprises and the expansion of existing enterprises to increase our total national income up to ninety or one hundred billion dollars. And still government officials pretend to wonder why business men don't go ahead in this country today.

And as the managers and investors of business are thus discouraged from going forward, it means fewer jobs in private industry for our unemployed. So, in terms of jobs these huge Federal expenditures and the building up of the national debt do affect the bread and butter of millions of our people, however ignorant they may be that Federal taxation affects them, for as President Roosevelt so well said in the 1932 campaign, taxes "are paid in the sweat of every man who toils." He might have added that in the long run a heavily taxed community is *never* a prosperous community.

And this invasion by the Federal government of the sources of revenue for support of local and state government is also an invasion of the ability of every employer of labor to pay wages and provide jobs. I have referred to the fact that while Governor Lehman has been paying off a ninety-four million deficit left by the administration of Governor Roosevelt, President Roosevelt in Washington is creating new and greater Federal deficits for future presidents to struggle with. It is being said that if the Federal government had not spent money in New York and other states that the states would have the deficit themselves. In other words, the Federal government has gone in the red in order to put the state governments in the black. This is a dangerous half-truth. It wholly ignores the question: Where did the Federal government get its money to spend in the state?

Despite any pretended sleight of hand, every dollar spent by the Federal government comes *from* states and from citizens in states. If rabbits are pulled out of the Federal hat, they were placed there by the states and their citizens. For example, the statement that expenditures by the Federal government took New York out of the red, wholly ignores the fact that in the fiscal years from 1933 to 1937 inclusive, the Federal government collected from the State of New York $3,388,000,000, and spent in that state for relief purposes only $1,545,000,000. So, every dollar spent by the Federal government *in* New York came *from* New York, or will come from New York in future taxation to pay off Federal bonds.

But this is not all. The figures show that for these four years the Federal government took from New York $1,843,000,000 which it did *not* spend in New York. On a per capita basis the Federal government collected from each man, woman, and child in New York State $262 and spent on them in relief $119 or $143 per capita less than it collected. In percentage the Federal government collected $100 from New York citizens and spent on them only $46.

Where did the rest of this New York money go? It was spent in other states. For example—during these four years from internal revenue collections the Federal government collected in North Dakota $6,000,000 but spent for relief purposes alone in that state $223,000,000, or $217,000,000 more than it collected. On a per capita basis the Federal government collected from the people of North Dakota $8.82 in four years and spent on them for relief purposes $318.07 or $310 per capita more than it collected. On a percentage basis the Federal government collected in North Dakota $100 and spent $3,600 whereas, in New York it collected $100 and spent $46.

The Federal government collected from every man, woman, and child in New York in addition to the $119 to be spent on New York citizens $143 to be spent on the citizens of other states.

Dealing as we are with the gradual destruction, the gradual drying up of sources of state revenues by the Federal government, it becomes an important question—what right has the Federal government to take per capita from the citizens of New York $143 (or for an average family of four $572 in four years) and spend it on the people in other states?

If the people in one section have the benefit of good climate, fertile soil, access to ocean navigation, etc., are the people in that locality not entitled to the benefit of these advantages?

If another section has the advantage of petroleum deposits or copper, or coal, are they not entitled to these advantages?

If the people in one section are thrifty and industrious, and the people in another section are indolent and lazy, why should the Federal government take from one and give to the other?

We are not discussing at the moment the question of disaster, or a great depression, or the human suffering in the wake of such depression. We are a generous people and have always responded to the claims of a common humanity. I am speaking at the moment of a process that goes on year after year, in good times and bad, of the Federal government reaching its taxing hand into the pockets of our people and taking wealth from the man who creates it and giving it to the man who does *not* create it. This has gone on year after year, but has become more noticeable in the last few years than at any previous time in the history of the republic.

To be wholly fair, it should be pointed out that these large discrepancies in Federal revenues from a certain state and Federal disbursements in the same state, are accounted for *in part* through the particular sources from which the Federal government obtains its revenue. North Carolina, for example, for many years paid into the Federal government in internal revenue taxes more money than any other state except New York, although it is not as large or wealthy a state as others, such as Illinois or Pennsylvania. This was due to the fact that the Federal government derives a substantial part of its revenue from excise taxes on tobacco. The home office of many of the great tobacco companies is in North Carolina and it is from that state, therefore, that the Federal government directly received so much of the tobacco tax. Similar situations prevail with respect to large corporate taxpayers resident in New York.

The North Carolina cigarette manufacturer, however, in turn collects the tax from the cigarette buyer in Nevada and North

Dakota. But after making all allowance for such considerations, they do not account for the tremendous discrepancies between collections and expenditures in the various states referred to above.

The man living in North Dakota, for example, certainly does not pay in indirect taxes on his cigarettes, or on any and all other commodities, the $310 per capita which represents the difference between what was collected by the Federal government in that state, and spent in that state.

But we are told that

"There must be no return to the practice and teaching that what an individual acquires should be his to dispose of as he sees fit."

No, Uncle Sam is going to decide that question for him. If Uncle Sam, with his great heart bleeding for mankind, decides the money could be spent more usefully for someone else—who did not earn it—it is to be taken from the man who did earn it.

The new definition of a humanitarian is "a politician who goes about doing good—with other people's money."

CHAPTER 12

CONSUMING THE STATES

"I see with the deepest affliction the rapid strides with which the Federal branch of our government is advancing towards the usurpation of all the rights reserved to the States, and the consolidation in itself of all powers, domestic and foreign; and that, too, by constructions which, if legitimate, leave no limits to their power."

—Jefferson.

Not only is the Federal government starving the wealth-producing states of the union, the tax-paying states, for the benefit of the tax-eating states, but it has begun a wholly new program and that is actually to take over, without the consent and against the strong opposition of state officials, the physical property—real estate—and other valuable property rights, lying within state boundaries.

As proof, I cite the Flood Control Bill passed on the day preceding adjournment of the last Congress. Governors and Senators from states as far removed as the states of Washington and Vermont, condemned this bill as—

"The opening wedge towards Federal ownership of all resources, including land, in all States."

"Would result to the State in loss of essential revenues."

"We are disturbed by constant encroachment by Federal authority in control of land, water and other resources."

"Would tend to give the Federal government title to the water resources of the States without their consent."

"Open way to Federal ownership and control of natural resources."

Until this bill was passed in the closing days of the last Congress, it had been the law that the Federal government could not go into a state and acquire property in that state,—land, water, minerals, etc., for flood control purposes, without the consent of the states. But by reason of an amendment offered by Senator Barkley of Kentucky, and without giving a public hearing to the states concerned, the Federal government asserts the right to consume the territory of the states with or without their consent.

It has been uniformly held by our highest courts that water and the valuable property rights in water for irrigation, reclamation, and power purposes, belong to the states in which the water is located. This was one of the advantages accruing to a state by virtue of a natural resource located therein. An upstream state, for example, had the first right to use water in that state to irrigate its own soil and build up its own prosperity. It could not be compelled, without its consent, to have dams erected in it and its valuable valley lands submerged and thus destroyed by reservoirs for the benefit of the downstream states.

But all this is now changed. Assuming that the bill passed in the last Congress is constitutional, or that it is in fact unconstitutional but that the Supreme Court of the United States can be *browbeaten* or "packed" to hold the contrary, the "consent of the governed" is no longer necessary. Because of the change of policy made in this bill it was described by Senator Austin of Vermont as—

> "The most shocking disregard of the rights of states that has ever occurred. I think it is the most significant change of our attitude toward a union of indissoluble states."

Senator Walsh said—

> "Is the Federal government to have the power to go into any state and seize by eminent domain any watershed, any water, any dams, and develop power without the state having any say whatever in the matter? . . . . Are

(the states) forbidden to have anything to say about the use of the power, cost of the power, the sale of the power, or the profit that may come from the power? . . . . We are dealing with an issue that goes right to the vitals of State rights. . . . . It ought not to be done in the closing days of Congress by an amendment revolutionizing the policy which has been pursued since the beginning of the government in dealing with the problem of flood control."

Senator O'Mahoney of Wyoming said—

"There will absolutely be taken from Wyoming all power to make any decision with regard to the distribution of water."

Under this bill, Vermont and New Hampshire, for example, or any upstream states having extremely valuable resources of flowing water, could not build a dam and develop power, and sell the power to the industries in other states, if the Federal government decided to take away these resources from the upstream state; and against the will of the upstream state and its people, distribute the benefit of these resources lying within that state to the people of other states.

Water, for example, in Wyoming, heretofore under the public control of that state for irrigation and reclamation projects for the benefit of their own citizens, and from which Wyoming, and its cities and towns would derive tax revenues for the support of schools and other public facilities, is no longer the property of Wyoming. That state is to be deprived of the control and distribution of its water to irrigate and reclaim its own land. Thus the control of the agricultural life and welfare of an entire state may be taken away from its own public officers and transferred to bureaucrats in Washington.

It was this feature of the Flood Control Bill, the destruction of the consent of the states, which President Roosevelt especially praised when he signed the bill. He said, "Insofar as this bill provides for an improvement in jurisdictional control over the properties involved, and a more adequate control over consequential power developments, it is a definite step in the right direction." Note that he said it was a "step."

The whole thing was summed up by Senator O'Mahoney in closing the debate. He stated that the bill says to the states—

"You are to be reduced from the status of sovereign states to that of mere satrapies of the Federal government, dependent for your progress not upon the efforts and energies of your own people, but upon the favors of Washington."

Under this bill, now the law of the land, to use one example out of many which might be given, the Federal government against the violent objection of the Governors and the people of the states of Vermont and New Hampshire, might take over the entire watershed in those states emptying into the Connecticut River, build dams, submerge their valleys, drive out their people, destroy or move the farm homes, schools, churches, and factories, and the towns and villages lying in the valleys; all without their consent, other than the forced consent implied in whatever sum might be awarded as damages in condemnation proceedings. (Assuming that courts will still be permitted to assess damages for property seized by the Federal government!) And, having taken over these peaceful valleys and driven out people who have lived there happily for generations, the Federal government would take from what is left of these states the tax revenues which they might have derived from the sale of power, or from their submerged fertile fields, and industries, and transfer all such revenues to Washington, D. C. "From him that hath not shall be taken."

Such is the new Federalism of an administration which professes itself to be the party of Thomas Jefferson! The party of States' Rights!

Nor is the Federal government to be hindered in its course by the fact that its huge expenditures, ostensibly for flood control—but in a large measure for the development of hydroelectric power, through the competition of hydro-electricity with coal—is depriving the coal miners of Pennsylvania, West Virginia, Kentucky, Indiana and Illinois, of their living. The coal states, the coal industries, and the coal miners are being taxed by the Federal government to build up competing hydro-electric projects to destroy the value of their coal! And so we have many abandoned coal towns!

It is an interesting sidelight that a couple of years ago, at the very time when there was a bill pending to spend another $300,000,000 to further develop the Tennessee Valley Authority, there was also pending a bill to spend $100,000,000 to buy up and take out of production coal mines for which there was no market.

And, as less coal is produced and hauled on the railroads, their situation becomes increasingly desperate. Such are a few of the effects in permanent damage to states, their industries, their agriculture, and the railroads serving them, arising from the super-Federalism now rampant in Washington. This chapter is entitled "Consuming the States"—and thus are the states literally being consumed.

And this is the way we are "solving" our problems "within the present framework of our form of government!"

CHAPTER 13

A WISE AND FRUGAL GOVERNMENT

"If we can prevent the government from wasting the labors of the people under the pretense of taking care of them, they must become happy."

"We must make our selection between economy and liberty or profusion and servitude."

"I consider the extravagance which has seized the country as a more painful evil than toryism was during the war. It is the more so as an example is set by the best and most amiable characters among us."

"The sacred preservation of the public faith I deem one of the essential provisions of our government and consequently one that ought to shape its administration."

"What more is necessary to make us a happy and prosperous people; still one thing more, *a wise and frugal government* . . . which shall not take from the mouth of labor the bread it has earned."

"The real credit of the United States depends on the ability and the immutability of their will to pay their debts."

—Jefferson.

"For three long years I have been going up and down this country preaching that government costs too much. I shall not stop that preaching. . . . I propose to use this position of high responsibility to discuss up and down the country at all seasons and at all times the duty of reducing taxes. . . . For three long years the Federal Government has been on the road toward bankruptcy. Too often in recent history liberal governments have been wrecked on the rocks of loose fiscal policy. We must avoid this danger. . . . The (Hoover) spending, my friends, is the most reckless and extravagant pace that I have been able to discover in the fiscal record of any peacetime government anywhere, any time. Taxes are paid in the sweat of every man who labors. If these taxes are excessive they are reflected in idle factories and tax-sold farms and in hoards of hungry people tramping the streets and seeking jobs in vain. Our workers may never see a tax bill but they pay it. They pay in deductions from wages, in increased cost of what they buy or (as now) in broad unemployment throughout the land. . . . Let us have the courage to stop borrowing to meet continuing deficits. Stop the deficits."

—Franklin D. Roosevelt.

We haven't stopped the deficits. We have been more reckless and more extravagant than ever. As a result we are now in our ninth consecutive year of deficits. The President has recently estimated the deficit for the present year (the 9th) at $3,984,-887,600, the highest for any New Deal year except 1936, when the soldiers' bonus was paid. The President now estimates an increase in the deficits for this year of $3,035,287,000 *more* than the estimate last January and tax revenues $919,130,000 *less* than the estimate last January. This is a "layman's budget." It excludes statutory debt retirement.

When John L. Sullivan was champion of the world he would walk into a crowded bar room and tell the barkeeper to "set 'em up for the boys." He was a "great guy." He probably would have received the unanimous vote of those present for any office in the gift of the people. When his money ran out he was no longer a "great guy."

I have been wholly unable to understand the complacency with which our citizens, and especially Democrats, view what was not so long ago described as "the road to bankruptcy." As

President Roosevelt himself has well said, in a time of emergency a person or a nation may borrow for a short period of time provided he then rigidly brings outgo within income. In that way he will have credit for the next emergency.

President Roosevelt also correctly said in March 1933—

> "Upon the unimpaired credit of the United States Government rests the safety of deposits, the security of insurance policies, the activity of industrial enterprises, the value of agricultural products, and the availability of employment. Credit of the United States Government definitely affects these fundamental human values."

In 1933 an emergency pump priming program of $3,300,-000,000 was adopted to finance public works. It is now argued that as we had recovery then, more of the same medicine will give us more recovery now. The conclusion does not follow. In 1933 we definitely set our faces toward putting our house in order. We reduced ordinary government spending. And from the standpoint of public confidence we did the very important thing of levying additional taxes for the express purpose of amortizing the $3,300,000,000 expenditure. We provided a sinking fund. Further, it was then expected that the emergency was temporary and we would soon be reducing the debt.

None of these conditions obtain today. The "emergency" no longer is temporary. We are not reducing ordinary expenses, we are increasing them, and we are not levying new taxes to amortize new expenditures. We are charging it "on the cuff." Pump priming in 1933 therefore is wholly different from the pump priming of 1938.

It might also be noted that the upsurge of business in 1933 began almost a year before the increased PWA expenditures began to flow out. In other words, the pump started to work *with confidence* without priming.

President Roosevelt, in the views he expressed in 1932 and 1933 was either right or wrong. If he was right at a time when the public debt was around 20 billion dollars, can he be right in holding an opposite view now that the debt is around 40 billion dollars?

There appears to have been a complete reversal of policy. In doing so there has been no greater repudiation of the teachings of Jefferson, Jackson, Cleveland, and many another who for over one hundred years gave character to the Democratic Party as the party committed to frugal government expenditure and consequent low taxation.

The dangers of our present course have been so clearly pointed out by President Roosevelt that little need be added to that point.

As, however, the "budget balancers" have now become an object of contempt by demagogues, it may be worth while to point out more clearly the way in which the "unimpaired credit of the United States Government does affect the safety of deposits, the security of insurance policies, the activity of industrial enterprises, the value of agricultural products and the availability of employment."

How does it affect the employment of labor? In the first place every dollar taken by taxation is a dollar less to be spent by the taxpayer whether he is a working man or an employer. When people go to the court house and pay their taxes of $50 or $100, they know that they have that much *less* to spend for employing labor to paint the house, or to buy next winter's coal, or to take a vacation. Every dollar which the *government* has *more* is a dollar that the *taxpayer* has *less*. There is an enormous amount of sophistry about the government "creating purchasing power." There is no way (except as I shall mention later) under which any government can "create" purchasing power—unless, perhaps, it is a government like Russia which operates all industry. In a country, however, in which property is privately owned, taxation does not create any purchasing power, it simply transfers it from one pocket to the other, from the pocket of the taxpayer to the pocket of the WPA worker, as an example. In the process, however, the total purchasing power of the nation has not increased a dime. Nor is the total possibility of the nation employing labor increased a dime. If government could "create" purchasing power, taxation and poverty and debt would all have been abolished centuries ago. No party would ever lose an election if it could "create" purchasing power.

The apparent exception to this statement is that when government borrows money and so spends more than it collects in taxes, it appears to create purchasing power, in the same way that a son who receives a mortgage-free farm from his father's estate might, by placing a mortgage on the farm, appear to have more purchasing power than he had without the mortgage. But all debts are a charge against future purchasing power. Government deficits of today are a charge against the purchasing power of our children. We are robbing the baby's bank to pay current bills.

Following the World War, for a period of eight or nine years in which the nation was more greatly prosperous than at any time before or since, even though much of it was fictitious, the government through taxation paid off the public debt created by the war at the rate of about one billion dollars a year. In other words, the earnings of the 1920-29 period went in part to pay the debt incurred in 1917-20. But over the entire period the war debts did not create any purchasing power. When debts are paid, any previous purchasing power is cancelled out, with interest.

In the same way, if we were again to begin to pay off the public debt, now increased since the low point more than twenty billion dollars, and do so at the rate of a billion dollars a year, it would take at least a quarter of a century of uninterrupted prosperity to liquidate the deficits plus interest incurred by the government since the depression began. As we cannot anticipate uninterrupted prosperity, nor continued peace, it is probable that fifty years will elapse before our debt is where it was in 1930.

It cannot be said, therefore, that over any long range period, government creates any purchasing power, or in the long run gives employment to labor as a result. But there is another way in which the continuance of an unbalanced budget definitely does curtail "the availability of employment." In planning future business, the erection of a new factory building, for example, the managers of that business must know, within some margin of predictability, what their future tax bill is going to be. If they are uncertain what their future tax bill is going to be, they hesitate to extend their plant and certainly investors hesitate to put their money into new extensions, because the tax collector always comes ahead of them. They get paid only if something is left.

Every business must anticipate its costs with some degree of certainty. If the budget of the Federal government were now balanced our business would have the assurance that taxes would not in the future be any higher than they are today. But with the continuance of an unbalanced budget there is no such assurance; on the contrary, there is the rather definite assurance that future taxes are going to be yet higher. And the uncertainty as to the amount of that future tax definitely chills the employment of labor. An unbalanced budget in France, long continued, has not made France prosperous. It has brought her almost to her knees financially and she has been forced to adopt the disturbing expedients of capital levies, repudiation by repeated devaluation of the franc, and forced loans. This does not create an atmosphere in which labor can look forward to steady employment. The proof of the pudding is in the eating thereof. The United States, after all these debts and deficits, *has two-thirds of all the unemployed of the whole civilized world.*

There are some 64 million life insurance policy holders, and millions of others having deposits in savings banks, building and loan associations and other forms of investment. These, too, were referred to by the President in March 1933. How does an unbalanced budget affect them? It affects them in this way:

Their deposits, the premiums that they have paid on their insurance have been reinvested in large part into promises of the government, that is, government bonds. Will these promises be paid by the government so that when the life insurance policy falls due it will, in turn, be paid by the company with dollars of substantially the same purchasing power as the dollars that the policy holder paid in?

With an unbalanced budget, long continued, all of these rights of the thrifty, frugal, sober, industrious part of our citizenship are at the hazard of the inability of the government to keep its promise, that is, to pay its bonds in dollars of equal purchasing power. There always comes a time when, if this process is long continued, no political party in power, responsible to the people at the next election, will have the courage to levy taxes sufficiently high to balance the budget, to bring income up to expenditures. When a government debt gets so high that the government can no longer levy taxes on the people sufficient to pay the debt (and still stay in office) printing press inflation or repudiation are then the only things left and such inflation is a species of repudiation. That is what we mean when we say that government expenditures have gotten "out of control." We are close to that point now. The people simply refuse to pay the bill. When this happens the middle class is wiped out. And when the middle class goes, the Man on Horseback comes. That is the danger of a continuing unbalanced budget. It is a threat to democracy itself, for when the frugal, thrifty, saving class of people are wiped out by inflation, repudiation, or capital levies, democracy has no friends left.

We are told, however, that new legislation provides controls which will prevent a "runaway inflation." Therefore we do not need to worry greatly over the fact that we are now in the ninth year of continuous deficits. If we examine these controls, however, we will see that they are like the brakes in an automobile driven by a man pursued by wolves. The controls may be there but they won't be used.

What are these controls which, *if the driver were free to use them,* would insure adequate protection against the danger of a ruinous inflation? Substantially there are five:

(a) Raising the Federal Reserve rediscount rate. This is supposed to curb credit inflation, that is, borrowing, by increasing interest rates; i.e., the cost of going into debt.

(b) Sale by the Federal Reserve Banks and their member banks of their holdings of government bonds on the open market, that is, to individual buyers. This is designed to reduce the supply of money and in so doing harden money rates which in turn would prevent credit inflation.

(c) Raising by the Federal Reserve Banks of the reserve requirements of member banks. This is intended to reduce excess banking reserves and thus reduce the available supply of bank credit and in turn prevent inflation.

(d) The upward revaluation of the dollar.

(e) The increase of margin requirements against brokers' loans in Stock Exchange buying. This is also designed to prevent "boom and bust."

The Administration, in my judgment, is entitled to very great credit in improving these controls, in the hope of leveling off the peaks and dips of the economic curve.

These controls appear adequate, but as a practical matter can they and *will they* be exercised while the government is still borrowing money, is still under the necessity of issuing more bonds, its budget still unbalanced?

If the rediscount rate is raised, and if as a result of expanding private business there is commercial paper seeking rediscount, the resulting increase in money rates would tend to drive down the price of government bonds carrying low interest rates. Banks would begin selling government paper yielding a per cent. or less and invest the proceeds in commercial paper paying a higher rate of interest. But this would jeopardize the government's financial operations. Its continuing deficits must still be financed by the issuance of *more* bonds and in addition the government would have to refund existing issues as they mature. Under such conditions the government could scarcely sell new bonds except at an increased interest rate as an inducement to the buyer, and as the government pays more interest on its bonds to the "coupon clippers" it in turn must increase its taxes which creates a political problem requiring superhuman courage on the part of government. It must levy increased taxes to pay increased interest to the "coupon clippers." I leave it to the reader how far a politically minded government would go down that road.

As government bonds paying a low rate of interest would begin to fall, as money rates on commercial paper rise, as a result of an inflationary boom and the attempt to control it by advancing the rediscount rate, the capital of banks and other large holders of government bonds would be threatened. There are banks today half of whose deposits are in government bonds. The government in turn has guaranteed these deposits. Neither the government nor the banks therefore can afford to see these bonds go below par. And it should be remembered that in 1932 government bonds were down as low as 83. With a 40 billion dollar debt, still growing, the man being chased by the wolves is scarcely in a position to increase the rediscount rate on commercial paper to check impending inflation.

The same reasoning applies to the sale by Federal Reserve Banks of their bonds in the open market to private buyers. Any large amount of selling of government bonds would tend to depress their price, and again the man chased by the wolves is not in a position to have bonds decline in value. How can he sell new bonds to meet new deficits when existing bonds are falling in value?

Increasing reserve requirements of Federal Reserve member banks also would seriously jeopardize the government's ability to continue to sell additional bonds to the banks whose reserve requirements had been increased and their investment ability decreased.

The fourth control, upward revaluation of the dollar (that

is, making gold worth in dollars less than the present price of $35 an ounce) as a mechanism to prevent wild inflation, is politically impossible, as it would involve enormous deflation of values, particularly agricultural commodity prices and would also involve serious international consequences for our foreign trade.

It will be seen, therefore, that the Federal government is not in a position to make effective use of these shiny new mechanisms for the control of inflation as long as it is under the constant necessity of finding additional markets for additional bond issues.

The use of inflation controls is prevented by the primary need of the government to protect the price, the market, and existing low interest rates on its bonds, and thus assuring the continued financing of a continuing deficit.

It will be seen, therefore, that *a balanced budget is the very heart* of the entire system of control of a ruinous inflation. With his budget balanced the man in the automobile could stop his car and begin shooting the wolves. Otherwise he cannot. He has nothing to do but to keep moving until his gas runs out.

When one reflects upon the fact that an increase of six hundred million dollars ($600,000,000) in bank reserves from 1922 to 1929 supported the enormous bank credit bubble of that period, and when it is seen that *"excess"* bank reserves today are, or soon will be, about $3,700,000,000, or more than six times that sum, the potentiality of serious inflation and real trouble becomes apparent. (Note: The "excess" reserves in 1928 were only $12,000,000, and in 1929 only $43,000,000.) We are gambling the credit of the government, the future of the currency, the solvency of the nation, "the safety of deposits, the security of insurance policies, the activity of industrial enterprise, the value of agricultural products, and the availability of employment," on the hope that no more "shots in the arm" will be necessary. As stated recently by Winthrop W. Aldrich, "This is, in effect, throwing away the brakes."

It is sufficiently serious if the man chased by the wolves is not able to use his brakes, but a downhill ride without brakes is bad enough without wolves!

Today's situation is charged with trouble. It is not to be passed off with a wisecrack. It has become a serious question whether our people are going to be led to their doom by the lure of easy money or whether they have sufficient intelligence and moral courage to stop further progress "on the road to bankruptcy."

Never in the history of this republic has there been greater need of public understanding of what Thomas Jefferson meant when he spoke of "a wise and frugal government . . . which shall not take from the mouth of labor the bread it has earned."

"Let us have the courage to stop borrowing to meet continuing deficits. Stop the deficits."

CHAPTER 14

THE PURGE COMES TO AMERICA

"I said (to President Washington) that if the equilibrium of the three great bodies—Legislative, Executive and Judiciary,—could be preserved, *if the Legislature could be kept independent*, I should never fear the result of such a government; but that I could not but be uneasy when I saw the Executive had swallowed up the Legislative branch."

—Jefferson.

A new doctrine is in the making and its consequences should be examined. They should be examined by men and women of all parties, but particularly by Democrats, for it is not a democratic doctrine.

It is that members of the executive branch of the Federal government may use the vast powers of their offices to nominate, elect or defeat candidates for Federal, state and local offices.

How does this square with our form of government? What legal, constitutional and moral standards are involved? What will be its effect upon our future?

The Constitution is a set of rules designed to help us live happily together. It has no other purpose. Read its noble Preamble. Whatever its failings it was emphatically not "a device for prevention of action," except such "action" as might endanger the rights of the citizens. There ought to be toward these rules an attitude of gallant sportsmanship. That attitude could be described as "constitutional morality." In tennis, baseball, boxing,—poker even—we call it "playing the game." In the code of sport it becomes a matter of honor. Its breach is met not with an intellectual disapproval alone, but with a moral condemnation. It holds men to their standards—so long as they are men.

In school, college, Y. M. C. A., Boy and Girl Scout work, Plattsburg training camps, etc., we teach youth to "play the game." We know the rules committee may change the rules next year, but this year we abide by this year's rules. To the player who deliberately "beats the gun," "cuts the corner," "hits below the belt," or, in other and plain words, cheats, we give the Bronx cheer. He soon goes.

We put the Christy Matthewsons and Walter Johnsons in the hall of fame, not only because they were superb athletes, but because they "played the game," and that is something that goes beyond the game itself. The great athlete who cheats is left out of the Valhalla of sports. He is not considered a sportsman. Look at the Chicago Black Sox as they passed to oblivion.

The moral value we assign to sports comes perhaps from a tacit recognition that *it is necessary to preserve the game itself*, for a game without rules is nothing. Even the youngest children recognize the necessity for rules in the games they invent. The morality of sport is instinctive.

CONSTITUTIONAL MORALITY

Is it less necessary in government? in human relations? in building prosperity? in improving our standards of living and maintaining our standards of life? Can we go on without rules and become a happy and prosperous people? Can we cheat the rules and still preserve the confidence by which men plan their futures? *A future without rules?* Can we build our house upon sand? Can we feel happy and secure in such a house?

This has become a question of very great consequence. Despite all talk at Washington of a "new moral climate," it can be demonstrated that on the part of important officials there has seldom, if ever, *been such a callous attitude toward con-*

stitutional morality, towards the rules which we as a people have adopted to regulate our living together.

This attitude is a complete reversal of Jefferson. He gave more than lip service to the Constitution. He did not think it was something to "get around." He did not, as he said, regard it as "a mere thing of wax." "To take a *single step* beyond the boundaries" that separated the functions of the Nation from the States, or the functions of the Executive, the Legislative and the Judiciary was to do something abhorrent and base. "With sincere zeal," he wished "an *inviolable preservation* of our present Constitution according to the true sense in which it was adopted by the States."

Let us contrast this constitutional morality of Jefferson with the attitude of New Dealers of the Corcoran-Cohen-Hopkins-Ickes-Williams variety. I mention these gentlemen especially because none of them, so far as I know, were ever members of the Democratic party.

In passing, it is not necessary to assume that these men have an evil purpose. Their motives may be the best. Let us assume that they are. They may think, sincerely, that their form of government is better than constitutional government. Mr. Hopkins, for example, although for years a registered Socialist, is doing his relief job as well as anyone could do it if it is to be done his way. As a welfare administrator in a Socialist state he would be entitled to high credit for disinterested and able service.

But motives—good or bad—fool us. A good motive is poor compensation for a bad result. Hell is paved with good intentions. These men, constitution-wise, are unmoral rather than immoral. Not being steeped in the American tradition, they may be wholly unaware what they are destroying. Perhaps they never read the Constitution. But if so, their ignorance does not save it. The unpardonable sin against democracy, as it is against God's law, is a state of mind in which a man doesn't know that he is doing wrong. Therefore, he cannot repent, and therefore, he cannot be pardoned.

THE TRADITION OF JEFFERSON

I am happy to say there are many in high office in Washington who scrupulously observe the boundaries of their jurisdictions. I refer to such men as Secretary Hull, Secretary Roper, Mr. Eastman of the Interstate Commerce Commission; Mr. Ayres of the Federal Trade Commission; Mr. McNinch of the Communications Commission; Mr. Douglas of the Securities Commission; Mr. Jones of the Reconstruction Finance Corporation, and scores of their associates.

These men exemplify the views of *Thomas Jefferson* when he was Secretary of State, as expressed by him in a letter to President Washington in 1792:

> "When I embarked in the government, it was with a determination to intermeddle not at all with the Legislature . . . As I never had the desire to influence the members (of Congress), so neither had I any other means than my friendships, *which I value too highly to risk by usurpation on their freedom of judgment,* and the *conscientious pursuit of their own sense of duty.*"

Would that we had more Jeffersons in Washington today! But to return to the Corcoran wing of the party, the promoters of the "purge." Their doctrine is that the government at Washington may seek to control, through its financial power and patronage, not only general elections, but even primary elections and conventions for nominating, and, therefore, controlling candidates for public office, not only at Washington, but in state capitols and city halls.

This doctrine, however disguised, is based on contempt for the people. Behind whatever mask, it is necessarily predicated on the view that the people in the states are *incapable of self-government,* or that Washington does not want their self-government. It is a species of treason toward *the very heart of democracy.* It is a *knife in the back* of the American Constitution.

It is a plan, or if not deliberately planned, it will have the inevitable effect of destroying the independence of Congress, and the independence of the States. I will go further and say it will destroy the States as such.

Let us see what a breach of constitutional morality this is. To begin with, of all the rights of the States,—and so of the human beings who live in the States—the independence of their electorate and the freedom of their elections is the most vital of all. From them is derived the "consent of the governed"—the heart of Democracy, if it is a free consent.

The State can exist as such only through its elections If it cannot control its own elections it cannot exist—*as a State.* Federal control of its ballot box, *if successful, will destroy it as a government, as surely as would an armed force sent out from Washington.*

This has been attempted before in our history, but it was bitterly opposed by democratic states and by the Democratic Party. But men calling themselves members of the party that once bitterly condemned it now do it—with self-approval.

THE FORCE ACTS

I refer to the Force Acts enacted to subject the South to the status of a conquered province of the Federal government, following the Civil War. These acts were passed ostensibly to "supervise" elections, but in fact to control elections, and those elected. Every Democrat in the Union denounced these acts as utterly unconstitutional. After twenty years of turmoil a Democratic president—Cleveland—and his Congress swept them from the statute books. These men knew that the right to vote comes from the State, not from Washington. They knew that whoever controls the voters controls the State. They knew that if Washington controls elections it will destroy our institutions and our Constitution. It will destroy state constitutions as well as the Federal Constitution. It will change the republic into a modern empire, with all the evils of ancient empires.

An attempt by the executive branch of the Federal Government to control the choice of Senators, is entirely destructive of the very structure, purpose and constitutional functions of the Senate. The same is equally true with respect to the House of Representatives.

RATIFICATION OF TREATIES

The Senate, for example, has the constitutional responsibility to ratify or *reject* treaties with foreign powers. This was designed by our fathers as a check against the evil consequences of a treaty negotiated by a rash or foolish president. But if Senators are the creatures of the president, because he, in effect, nominated and elected them, this function of the Senate is destroyed—the safeguard is gone. Only the shadow remains. The Senate then speaks the will of the president and not their own will, or the will of their people. And his will is, of course, *that the treaty be ratified!*

Do the people—do you—*want this safeguard abolished?* The power to reject a treaty, a foreign entanglement?

IMPEACHMENT

To the House of Representatives is given the constitutional responsibility of impeaching a president. To the Senate is given the constitutional duty of trying the impeachment. It was a safeguard set up by our fathers to save themselves—to save *you* —from tyranny,—the usurpation of power by a president. Although presidential impeachment has occurred only once, nevertheless the power is there, and so long as the power remains it necessarily influences conduct like a gun behind the door, even though not used.

But the power is futile unless Senate and House are free to exercise the power. And this they cannot be if they owe their nomination and election to the president. It would be like a defendant at the bar naming the jurors to try him.

Do the people—do you—want this safeguard abolished? The power to impeach and remove a president who has betrayed the public trust?

ELECTION OF PRESIDENT

To the House of Representatives is given the constitutional duty, under certain circumstances, to elect the President of the United States. This is when no candidate for that office receives a majority of the Electoral College vote. In that case the House of Representatives elects the president, each state delegation voting under the unit rule, and each state having one vote, 25 states thus electing the president.

This has happened once in our history and is always possible when there are three parties in the field, as in 1912 or 1924. In 1912 Mr. Taft was president, and was seeking reelection. If Mr. Wilson had received less than half the electoral vote, the House of Representatives by a vote of its delegations in 25 of the smallest states might have reelected Mr. Taft, although he had received, as he did, less than one-third of the total popular vote, and had thus been repudiated by the people.

The danger of a repudiated president continuing in office, when the election is thrown into the House of Representatives, would be immensely increased if Congressmen from 25 small states owed their election to him, through his "blank check" control of billions of dollars. A special session of the Congress could be called after the November election. This session could require the electoral vote to be at once cast, showing no candidate had a majority of that vote, and then proceed to elect a president. *Thus a defeated Congress could constitutionally reelect a repudiated president.*

Admittedly this danger is remote but if it ever occurred it would confront the nation with a very grave crisis, possibly civil war, and if not war, four years of turmoil and panic.

Our fathers intended the House of Representatives, in such case, to be free men not the puppets of the sitting president.

Do the people—do you—want this safeguard abolished?

CONFIRMATION OF NOMINATIONS

To the Senate is given the power to confirm or reject nominations of Federal judges, foreign ambassadors, cabinet officials, etc. Destroy this power and a president contemptuous of our Constitution could fill the courts with puppets equally contemptuous of the Constitution. A president who hated Catholics, or Jews, or Negroes, or other racial or religious minorities, or who hated Labor, or private property, *or who hated States,* could fill the courts with judges who had the same hatreds.

Does Labor, for example, want to be helpless in resisting the confirmation of a judge on the United States Supreme Court, for the reason that they believe he favors "yellow dog" contracts? But that may be the price Labor will sometime pay if it assists in destroying the independence of Senators.

Many other instances could be given. Again, the power to reject nominations, even though seldom exercised, must always be a restraining influence for good in the selection of these important public officials. But if Senators are the tools of the president, the power given *them* by our fathers passes to the president, and so the power to protect free institutions—and to protect you—vanishes.

Do the people—do you—want this safeguard abolished?

Do the people—do you—for example, want the entire power to handle foreign relations, the naming of ambassadors and the making of treaties to rest in the hands of *one man?* But that is what, practically, is done if Senators are no longer free to vote their honest convictions on the confirmation of nominations or the ratification of treaties, because they owe their offices and votes to the president.

WAR

Let us take this one step further—war. To check an unwise or ambitious or impetuous president, our fathers placed in the hands of Congress alone the sole power to declare war and to appropriate funds for its prosecution, if declared. It is clear that it was intended that this awful responsibility—far more awful now than 150 years ago, because war is far more awful— was to be exercised by free men—free from the controlling power and pressure of the president. But make Congressmen and Senators the puppets of the president and this power to save a great nation from the frightful consequences of an unwise and unwanted modern war becomes emasculated. It becomes worthless. It ceases to be a power. It is like an egg that has been sucked by a weasel.

Do the people—do you—want this safeguard abolished?

I do not know your views with respect to the "Ludlow Resolution" to amend the Constitution to require direct popular consent before engaging in foreign war. You may be, for it or against it. The proposed amendment may have been wise or not. But in either event it illustrates the danger of the new doctrine —the new immorality—the view that Senators and Congressmen must do the will of the president, and if not, he may use, unlawfully, the vast powers of his great office to retire them from public life.

Let it be noticed that the Administration defeated the Ludlow Resolution. That means that it did not want the people to decide when, and under what circumstances they would fight in Europe or Asia. It could mean nothing else. But if the people are to be denied this *direct* power to protect the bodies of their sons then it must be plain that the *people's representatives* must have this power. Otherwise, the people have *no protection whatever* against the rashness of a hot-headed president, or the *secret* pressures of powerful interests concentrated upon the White House or the Secretary of State.

The Constitution attempted to so protect the people—to protect you—by leaving this power in the people's representatives—men free to vote their will, and your will, and not the president's will—your men and not "King's men." *But the purge, if it succeeds, will destroy this one protection you have against being led to slaughter on foreign fields by foolish or ambitious men. Such is the cost of one-man or one-party government. Such is the price of the purge.*

Do the people—do you—want to pay this price of one-man government,—"tyranny," Thomas Jefferson called it,—whether that one man be the present President of the United States or any future president,—*whoever he may be?* Because it must be plain that the purge, if once recognized as a legitimate political weapon, *will not be willingly relinquished in the future.* If you do not want to pay this price, you fathers and mothers and wives of the men of America, resist this new immorality, prevent this purge as you would prevent a pestilence. Insist that *your representative* in Congress be a free man, and vote *against* any candidate for that high office who has been obviously selected by the promoters of the purge and promises to be subservient to them.

CHAPTER 15

SHALL WE DESTROY CONGRESS?

When you destroy the free exercise of a constitutional function of the Congress, to that same extent you destroy the Congress, and the Constitution which created it. When you destroy the independent exercise of a constitutional function of the Congress or of the states, or of the cities, counties, or townships, to that extent you destroy the thing itself.

Every separation of power was intended by our fathers to prevent the abuse of power. The "checks and balances" of our "antiquated" Constitution had only one purpose,—*to protect you and your children* against the unwise use or the abuse of concentrated power. It was to limit the damage inherent in the abuse of power—like a fire wall in a building, an asbestos curtain in a theatre, or a bulkhead in a ship.

It is apparent that if the humblest office of the Federal government may be used to influence an election anywhere, then all its offices and all their functions, moneys, forces, resources, and powers may be used everywhere to influence elections. The only restraint would be whether "you could get away with it." And this despite the fact that no one in the executive branch has the slightest vestige or scintilla of constitutional power to nominate or elect a single Senator, Congressman, Governor, or Mayor anywhere. There is not a shred of legal or moral right to do so. It is a power which does not rightfully or constitutionally belong to the Executive.

The whole careful design of constitutional checks and balances to be exercised by free men absolutely precludes any thought that the president or those under him might use his office to nominate or elect these officials and so destroy their freedom. Caesar selecting his pro-consuls to rule the most distant parts of his empire was not the model used by Washington and his compeers in framing the Constitution.

VOTING—A STATE FUNCTION

If anything further were needed to demonstrate how utterly unconstitutional this new doctrine is, it would be further shown by the fact that the right and privilege to vote is a privilege *granted by states,* and not by the Federal government. It is a matter wholly within the constitutional control of the several states, subject only to the provisions of the Federal Constitution, that the voting privilege may not now be withheld by a state on account of race, color, previous condition of servitude, or sex.

Any state, however, could require a legal voter to be 30 years of age rather than 21, or not over 60, or could debar anyone not a native born citizen, or could require one to be able to read and write, or to own so much property or pay so much taxes, etc., in order to vote. A state, for example, could provide that presidential electors be chosen by the governor, or by the state legislature, rather than by vote of the people.

All this illustrates one point only, that "the right to vote in the State comes from the State" and "the United States has no voters in the states of its own creation" as held time and again by the United States Supreme Court. *Hence it is clear as sunlight that the Federal government has no lawful right to influence or control elections, or voters, or votes in the states, for any office whatever.* To do so is as much an invasion of their rights, and hence of the rights of their people, as to seize their statehouse with Federal troops. To admit in any power other than its own people a dominion over its elections is to place the State itself under such dominion.

When the Federal Executive or any of his agents or through moneys at his or their disposal seek to nominate, or elect, or defeat the mayor of a city, the governor of a state, or its Senator, Congressman, member of its electoral college or any other officer, it is to destroy statehood itself.

DESTRUCTION OF CIVIL RIGHTS

It has been often said recently that however far the Federal government may extend its economic power it will scrupulously safeguard the "civil rights" of the citizen.

Don't worry. Nothing will happen to those precious rights! We will protect them! Leave it to us!

But it must be noted that the *greatest and most important civil right of all* is the right of the citizen to vote his unbought and unfrightened judgment on matters concerning his own government. From this civil right all other rights depend,— freedom of worship, freedom of the press, trial by jury, etc., etc. When the right to cast a free ballot is gone the power to defend these other rights is gone also. And when the power to defend rights is gone the rights themselves go also!

SHALL CONGRESSMEN BE EXPELLED?

Who has in truth the sole right to make a free choice of Senators and Congressmen if not their own constituencies? This has come up many times in election contests, especially those involving the right of national political minorities to *have* representatives even from districts where they are in the majority. For example, the Victor Berger case from the Milwaukee district during the World War, or the State Assembly at Albany voting to exclude Socialist members, an action which former Governor Hughes vigorously condemned.

By express constitutional provision each House of the National Congress "shall be the judge of the elections, returns and qualifications of its own members." Strictly construed this would seem to give the House or Senate the power to exclude any one not "qualified," if his political, or social, or economic views are abhorrent to the majority, whether he is considered a "wild man" or a "copperhead." Yet in cases such as those to which I have referred it has always been contended that it would be a grave breach of the most sacred right of self-government to deny to any constituency the representative of their free choice, if otherwise legally elected and qualified.

But suppose the purge is directed against such a candidate. And suppose a majority of his constituents vote for him notwithstanding, as they did for Congressman Victor Berger. What then? Is the purge to continue? *Are persons in the executive branch to urge the Senate and House to deny the elected candidates his seat? And is that vote to exclude to be made a question of loyalty to the one-party super-state? And if Senators and Congressmen defy the wish of the mighty, and vote to seat the undesired candidate, are they themselves to be the next victims of the purge?*

Are these questions fanciful? This I must leave to you in the light of the purge doctrine as exemplified by its devotees abroad. Certain it is that no self-imposed limits have so far been placed on the purge. All we know now is that the power to purge is asserted, and power seldom places limitations on its own use.

FREE AND INDEPENDENT STATES

Once it was proclaimed that "these Colonies are, and of Right ought to be, Free and Independent States."

Free and independent of whom? Of the British Crown alone? No, free and independent of every one, present or future, except those to whom they voluntarily gave power or allegiance.

Later the Constitution said the same thing by providing that the "powers not delegated to the United States . . . are reserved to the States, respectively, or to the people."

The power to nominate or elect public officials has not been delegated to the United States, or to any person holding office under the United States. No such official has any power not conferred by the Constitution. It follows, therefore, that any effort by a Federal official to use *the power of his office* to influence or control elections is *exercised unconstitutionally*.

Let us not be confused in this matter. It may be said, and correctly, that we have party government; that the president is a party man, generally, although not necessarily the most influential member of his party; that a president may, and has for many years, participated in elections and urged the election to office of members of his party.

All this is freely granted. But it does not lead to the conclusion that Senators, Congressmen, governors and mayors owe allegiance to the president. They owe allegiance to the Constitution. As party men they also unofficially owe support to the platform of the convention, the decision of the caucus, and the historic principles of their party.

But beyond this their allegiance does not go. They are not "King's men." They are not "rubber stamps." No Federal official has any lawful power to reduce them to rubber stamps. No one has the official right to select rubber stamps. No one has the constitutional power to attempt to drive from public office those who refuse to be rubber stamps.

There may be a twilight zone where it is difficult to tell when day ends and night begins. But from the fact that this difficulty exists no one can prove that day is night, or night, day. There is a point at which influence ends, and coercion begins.

Where is this point? It seems plain that the legitimate influence which a man who happens to be president, or an official under him, may exercise in an election, is measured by such resources of character and leadership as he may possess *as a man*, but not *as an official*. If, for example, he is a strong public speaker, or has radio technique, or appears to advantage on the silver screen, he has more power to persuade voters and influence elections than one devoid of these qualities.

But when he uses powers which *his office* gave him, which he would not possess *except for the office*, there is no constitutional warrant for such use. If a president, for example, as Commander-in-Chief of the army and navy, sends troops to the polling place, as was done under the Civil War Force Acts, to intimidate voters, it would be a tyrannical act. If he uses public moneys to bribe the electorate or a single voter, it is a breach of constitutional morality, as well as a penal offense. *If by virtue of his office,* any one in the executive branches does or says anything designed to coerce or control or put under duress or fear or hope of financial gain, the humblest voter, he has gone beyond the powers of that office.

THE FEDERALIST PAPERS

"Whose bread I eat, his song I sing" was not what our fathers had in mind when they went to such pains—for us—to make state and national government, and the different departments of government independent of control, each by the other. If one cannot perceive the distinction here drawn he is incapable of understanding our Constitution, and unworthy to hold office under it. As the Federalist Papers put it,—

> "Though it might be allowable to suppose that the Executive might occasionally influence some individuals in the Senate, yet the supposition that he could in general *purchase the integrity of the whole body,* would be forced and improbable."

With respect to the wisdom to require nominations to be confirmed by the Senate, the Federalist says that not only will it

> "be impracticable to the Executive to corrupt or seduce a majority of its numbers,"

but, in turn, the Senate by the power to reject a nomination, will exert

> "a salutary restraint upon the conduct of that magistrate"

against nominating to high public office those

"personally allied to him, or possessing the necessary insignificance and pliancy to render them the obsequious instruments of his pleasure."

With respect to the necessary independence of the Senate to try an impeachment, the Federalist says:

"What other body would be likely to feel *confidence enough in its own situation* (their italics) to preserve unawed and uninfluenced, the necessary impartiality between an individual accused, and the *Representatives of the People, His Accusers?*"

With respect to the power of the Senate to ratify *or reject* treaties with foreign nations which under the Constitution become the supreme law of the land, the Federalist, remarking upon *"that love of fame, the ruling passion of the noblest minds,"* says:

"An ambitious man might make his own aggrandizement, by the aid of a foreign power, the price of his treachery to his Constitution. The history of human conduct does not warrant that exalted opinion of human virtue which would make it wise in a nation to commit interests of so delicate and momentous a kind, as those which concern its intercourse with the rest of the world, to the sole disposal of a magistrate created and circumstanced as would be a President of the United States."

And, finally, what was the view of the Federalist on this whole matter of one-man, or one-party government? It was this:

"The accumulation of all powers, legislative, executive and judiciary, in the same hands, whether of one, a few, or many, and whether hereditary, self-appointed, or elective, may *justly be pronounced the very definition of tyranny.*"

CENTRALIZATION AND CORRUPTION

Jefferson's fear that "if ever this country is brought under a single government, it will be one of the most extensive corruption" and "as venal and oppressive as the government from which we separated," ought to be reread by the present administration and by every administration.

I here quote some scattered excerpts from the recent debate in the United States Senate when administration leaders successfully voted down every effort to punish the use of Federal relief funds to influence elections:

SENATOR WHEELER (reading an Associated Press dispatch from Des Moines, Iowa):

> "J. T. Jones, executive assistant of the Iowa National Emergency Council, asserted President Roosevelt 'should have the right to define and have voice in the election of the men he needs to assist him. It develops that Otha D. Wearin is preferred for the Senatorial post. Therefore, the good soldier will say, "I'm for Wearin.'"

SENATOR BAILEY:

> "Last year when we were engaged in the battle over the Judiciary bill . . . who went to the radio and appealed to the American people but this Administrator Hopkins . . . the man whom we trust to distribute billions of dollars goes to the radio and makes an appeal for the support of the bill. . . . When he made the declaration the other day for the candidate in Iowa he knew exactly what he was doing. I give him credit for having that much sense. . . . When LaGuardia was running for Mayor in New York who went and pointed out the public works there, and asked the New York people to vote for LaGuardia? Who did that but Mr. Harold Ickes, 'Honest Harold'? . . . The people understand it perfectly."

SENATOR BARKLEY:

> "I am willing to concede that Mr. Hopkins was guilty of an indiscretion in making that statement . . . but I do not admit that as a matter of principle, Mr. Hopkins was guilty of any more of an indiscretion because he spends the money than we who appropriate it."

SENATOR McCARRAN:

"Does not the Senator distinguish between those who merely appropriate and have no power of paying out, and the one who has absolute control and pays out directly to the dependent and the needy?"

SENATOR BARKLEY:

"Oh, I grant there is a theoretical distinction."

SENATOR CHAVEZ:

"The average governor is looking to a seat in the United States Senate. That is the practical side of the matter. If we adopt the pending amendment the result will be to hurt a Senator such as the Senator from Kentucky."

SENATOR BARKLEY:

"They (state employes) are at liberty to roam around at their will or the will of their boss or their organization and indulge in politics to their heart's content, but we are proposing that anybody connected with a job under WPA or PWA or CCC or AAA or any other activity for which we appropriate money in this joint resolution (the three billion dollar spending-lending bill) shall be tied with a rope to a tree so he is helpless and cannot even speak, unless he can whisper in the ear of somebody what his convictions are while these others (e.g., workers on Federal aid highways under state administrations) who draw pay out of the Treasury of the United States are free to roam at will and play the political game to their heart's content."

SENATOR McCARRAN:

"We are dealing with a thing that means much to American life. We are either going forward with a great democracy or we are going down. . . . Today how many are there in America whose meal ticket is controlled by some Federal agency. . . . The whole question is, Shall the people rule or shall someone who has been delegated by the people to minister to the needs of the unemployed, the lowly and humble, dominate them so that by reason of necessity, growing out of a colossal depression, the *unfortunate shall yield their free will to the dominating force of money?"*

THE ISSUE BEFORE US

There is the question, nobly and tersely stated by Senator McCarran. It is a question whether we should permit Federal officials to coerce voters to *"yield their free will to the dominating force of money."* Shall Hinky Dink and Bathhouse John be the models for Washington officials? The next question is whether the people will back up men like McCarran, Wheeler, Austin, George, Byrd, Bailey, Van Nuys, Vandenberg, Burke, etc. If not, the purge goes on, these men and men like them go out, and rubber stamps go in.

DECENTRALIZE RELIEF

Nothing better illustrates the dominant note of Jefferson's philosophy than the certain evils of relief administered from Washington. It is of imperative importance that relief be decentralized, administered by local agencies, responsible to local taxpayers, even though the Federal government contribute to the cost, as in fact, seems necessary.

I am not unaware of the existence of local political machines as well as Federal political machines. Unfortunately there are opportunities for waste, loss and graft in the disbursements of public funds however handled. "Where the meat hangs, there the wolves gather." And "with money we will get men, and with men, we will get money," as Cæsar said.

But it is infinitely to be preferred that such evils be localized. It will be less to begin with, and it will do much less harm. It will not be used to control Congressmen and Senators in framing policies for 130,000,000 people which will destroy our Constitution. Far better an occasional "rotten borough" than a rotten Republic.

INDEPENDENCE OF CONGRESS

The American people are willing to grant the central government at Washington whatever powers are reasonably necessary to deal with problems which, in good faith, are national in their scope, and which are beyond the effective solution of governments of the states, but only on one great condition. That condition is that the people's Congress shall remain free as the great policy determining agency of 130,000,000 people, to pass on public questions on their merits, and that the people themselves remain free to cast an independent and unpurchased and unpurchasable ballot on election day.

If, however, Congress is no longer a free agent, its freedom impaired or destroyed by the implied threat to grant or withhold a sewer system or a highway in the Congressman's home district, and if the people, for similar reasons, are no longer free to vote for free representatives, because the power over the purse has passed from their own hands, then democracy here in America has entered the twilight. If democracy goes by the board in our own dear land, as it has in bloodstained lands beyond the seas, the monument to that great lost cause will be erected on Capitol Hill.

On June 25th at Flat River, Missouri, Senator Bennett Champ Clark stated his conception of public trust and congressional independence as follows:

"Whenever the people of Missouri arrive at the conclusion that it is part of the duty of a United States Senator to agree sight unseen upon any policy as to which the Congress knows nothing, then I will no longer solicit their support for public office."

As government policies more and more affect the daily life of our citizens, it is becoming of increasing importance for the people to decide whether they want political Charley McCarthys in office, or men whose public attitudes are determined by the quality of *intellectual integrity which Senator Clark has so well described*.

As long as Congress is free, and the people are free, they can cure their own mistakes in free elections every two or four years. No mistake then becomes final. No evil then is without remedy. No deviation from democracy then becomes destiny.

Relief should be administered by local or state governments and it should be a criminal offense for a Congressman or Senator to recommend by word or writing an applicant for any form of relief job. Many men on Capitol Hill would thank God if that were the law today.

Nor need any person worthy of relief fear the result of such a program. It might well be that as the political hitch hikers are dropped, the amount per person to the needy would be increased. Certainly there is nothing to argue that it would be less.

Unless some such program is adopted, the great rights of all American citizens will be whittled away. Every one of these rights is a safeguard to protect liberty, property, reputation and person. For centuries men of our race died on the battlefield, or in prison, or on the gibbet, or under the axe, or were burned alive in order to secure these rights, to control their own elections, and through those elected to govern themselves; to ratify or reject treaties; to confirm or refuse to confirm judges, ambassadors, and other important officials; to elect presidents; to impeach them; to decide whether they shall go to war; to govern themselves.

Every one of these rights, and many more, secured to the people by the Constitution of the United States, or by the constitution of their own states, is gradually being undermined, taken away, abolished. And the people are not aware that it is being done! Or are they?

THE VIEWS OF PRESIDENT WASHINGTON

How George Washington would have regarded the "purge" is shown by a remarkable letter written by him when he was president of the United States. Added significance comes from the fact that it was written only a few weeks before he was, for the second time, elected president by the unanimous vote of the Electoral College, an honor that has come to no other American.

The letter is dated September 26, 1792. It was written to John Francis Mercer, a candidate for reelection to Congress. Some of Mercer's friends had implied that President Washington was favorable to his election. When the President heard this he wrote a letter directly to Mercer, from which I quote:

"I come now to another part of your letter, and in touching upon it, do not scruple to declare to you that I was not a little displeased to find by a letter from Captn. Campbell, to a gentleman in this neighborhood, that my name had been freely used by you or your friends for electioneering purposes, when I had never associated your name and the election together; and when there had been the most *scrupulous and pointed caution* observed on my part, not to express a sentiment respecting the fitness or unfitness of any candidate for representation that could be construed, by the *most violent torture of the words,* into an interference in favor of one, or to the prejudice of another.

"Conceiving that the exercise of an influence, (if I really possess any) however remote would be *improper; as the people ought to be entirely at liberty to chuse whom they pleased to represent them in Congress.* Having pursued this line of conduct steadily, my surprise and consequent declaration can be a matter of no wonder. . . .

"I instantly declared to the person who showed me the Letter;—'that to the best of my recollection, I never had exchanged a word to, or before Bushrod Washington on the subject of your election, much less to have given such a decided opinion. That such a measure would have been incompatible with the rule I had prescribed to myself, and which I had *invariably observed,* of not interfering *directly or indirectly,* with the suffrages of the people, in the choice of their representatives. . . .' "

Such was the position, "invariably observed," of the man who presided over the convention that wrote the Constitution of the United States. No better authority can be cited; no stronger character ever held public office; no one ever better understood, and was more determined to preserve our form of government.

His position on the "entire liberty of the people" to choose "whom they pleased to represent them in Congress" is to be contrasted with that of the promoters of the purge.

WE RETURN TO JEFFERSON

It was soon to be the Fourth of July, 1826,—the 50th anniversary of the Declaration of Independence. In the intervening years 53 of the 56 signers had died. Only three remained,—Adams of Massachusetts, Carroll of Maryand, and Jefferson of Virginia. But on the golden anniversary of the great Declaration, by an almost supernatural coincidence, Adams and Jefferson were to join the immortals. Only Carroll was destined to survive.

But the Declaration itself was not dead nor dying. It still lived in the hearts of the people. Soon they were to hear it read again from the village green, from the tree stump in the wilderness. Soon they were to hear again:

"He has conspired with others to subject us to a jurisdiction foreign to our Constitution and unacknowledged by our laws."

"Suspending our own Legislatures, and declaring themselves invested with power to legislate for us in all cases whatsoever."

"He has made Judges dependent on his Will alone, for the tenure of their offices, and the amount and payment of their salaries."

"For resisting with manly firmness his invasions on the rights of the People."

"Altering fundamentally the Forms of our Government."

"All having in direct object the establishment of an absolute Tyranny over these States—to prove this let Facts be submitted to a candid world."

But the man who wrote these words was dying at Monticello. As the shadows gathered around him his mind went back fifty years to the events of his young manhood. His fingers moved as if he were writing. Suddenly he spoke, startling those at his bedside, "The Committee of Safety—it ought to be warned."

CHAPTER 16

THE CONSTITUTION AND THE COURTS

"As independent or separate nations, a spirit of forebearance and compromise therefore, and not of encroachment and usurpation, is the healing balm of such a constitution; and each party must prudently shrink from all approach to the line of demarcation instead of rashly overleaping it, or throwing grapples ahead to haul to thereafter."

"To take a single step beyond the boundaries thus specifically drawn around the power of Congress, is to take possession of a boundless field of power, no longer susceptible of any definition."

"Our peculiar security is in the possession of a written Constitution. Let us not make it a blank paper by construction."

—Jefferson.

The Supreme Court Bill and the Executive Reorganization Bill have been so recently and widely discussed that it is not necessary to refer to these measures at length. It is appropriate only to discuss them briefly in the light of Jeffersonian principles. Recent efforts to build up Jefferson as a precedent for the Court packing and the Executive Reorganization Bill as it was originally drafted are a libel on history.

It can be stated categorically that Jefferson—

a. Believed in constitutional government which is a government that restrains governors;
b. Believed in the checks and balances of three separate branches of government, each operating to prevent the abuse of power by the other;
c. Believed in the independence of the judiciary;

124

  d. Opposed the concentration of power in the executive;
  e. Did not countenance forced or strained constructions
     of the Constitution.

The following excerpts from his writings are proof of the foregoing:

"An elective despotism was not the government we fought for, but one which should not only be founded on free principles, one in which the powers of government should be so divided and placed among several bodies of magistracy as that no one could transcend their local interests without being effectually checked and restrained by the others.

"I suppose an amendment to the Constitution necessary by consent of the States because the objects now recommended are not among those enumerated in the Constitution."

"The dignity and stability of government in all its branches, the morals of the people and every blessing of society depend so much on an upright and skillful administration of justice that the judicial power ought to be distinct from both the legislative and executive and independent from both that so it may be a check upon both as both should be checks upon that. The judges . . . should not be dependent upon any one man or body of men. To these ends they should hold estates for life in their offices, or, in other words their commissions should be during good behavior and their salaries ascertained and established by law.

"Confidence is everywhere the parent of despotism—free government is founded in jealousy and not in confidence; it is jealousy and not confidence that prescribes limited constitutions to bind down those whom we are obliged to trust with power. Our Constitution has accordingly fixed the limits to which, and no further, our confidence may go. Let the honest advocate of confidence read the alien and sedition acts and say that the constitution has not been wise in fixing limits to the government it created and whether we should be wise in destroying these limits. . . . In questions of power, *let no more be heard about confidence in man but bind him down from mischief by the chains of the constitution.*

"They would, indeed, consider such a rupture (separation of the states) as among the greatest calamities which could befall them; but not the greatest. There is one greater, submission to a government of unlimited powers.

"This commonwealth is determined, as it doubts not its Co-States are, to submit to undelegated and consequently unlimited power in no man or body of men on earth.

"The several states composing the United States of America are not united on the principle of unlimited submission to their General Government but that by a compact under the style and title of a Constitution for the United States and amendments thereto they constituted a General Government for special purposes—delegating to that government certain definite powers, reserving each state to itself the residuary mass of right to their own self government and that whensoever the General Government assumes undelegated powers its acts are unauthoritative, void and of no force . . . the Government created by this compact was not made the exclusive or final judge of the extent of the powers delegated to itself since then we have made its discretion, and not the Constitution, the measures of its powers.

"If we have a doubt relative to any power we ought not to exercise it. When we consider the extensive and deep-seated opposition to this assumption; the conviction entertained by so many that this deduction of powers by elaborate construction prostrates the rights reserved to the States; the difficulties with which it will rub along in the course of its exercise; that changes of majorities will be changing the system backwards and forwards so that no undertaking under it will be safe; that there is not a state in the union which would not give the power willingly by way of amendment, with some little guard, perhaps, against abuse; I cannot but think it would be the wisest course to ask an express grant of the power."

This should be contrasted with the letter of President Roosevelt to Congressman Samuel B. Hill with respect to the then pending Guffey Coal Bill, in which the President expressed the hope that members of Congress would not permit their doubts however reasonable with reference to the constitutionality of the measure to prevent their passing the bill.

Jefferson was not a blind worshiper of the courts or of the Constitution. Nor should we be. The Constitution was made to serve men, and as Jefferson said, "The earth belongs to the living." He knew "that laws and institutions must go hand in hand with the progress of the human mind." The courts are but the instruments to see that government officials keep within the rules which the people themselves have laid down.

Jefferson, it cannot be too often said, was in favor of giving to the general government whatever powers are actually necessary and which cannot be competently exercised in other hands. On at least one occasion he urged an amendment to the Constitution to grant the general government additional power. With respect to the Louisiana Purchase he did not pretend that he believed its purchase was within the power of the chief executive, or of the Federal government. On the contrary, he frankly and honestly stated that he did not think the United States under the Constitution had the power to purchase foreign territory. He acted with respect to the Louisiana territory only in an emergency to prevent the land from being sold by Napoleon into other hands. He fully anticipated that Congress would submit to the people of the United States an amendment to the Constitution which would, if adopted, ratify and confirm the purchase. Jefferson himself prepared a draft of an amendment to accomplish this result.

Jefferson's conduct in this matter was exactly similar to that of an agent working for his principal. Knowing that with respect to some pressing matter he does not have the granted power to act, nor time to obtain it, he acts on his own responsibility. If his act is later approved by his principal, subsequent ratification is just as effective as previous authorization. Jefferson said expressly, "The constitution has made no provision for our holding foreign territory, still less for incorporating foreign nations into our Union. The Executive . . . has done an act beyond the Constitution." "I pretend," he said to Congress, "no right to bind you. You may disavow me and I must get out of the scrape as I can. I thought it my duty to risk myself for you. But we shall not be disavowed by the nation and their act of indemnity will confirm and not weaken the constitution by more strongly marking out its lines."

The fact that Congress did not deem it necessary to obtain by constitutional amendment an express ratification of Jefferson's purchase of Louisiana, cannot diminish Jefferson's candid interpretation of his acts in the matter. Jefferson did not resort to strained constructions of the Constitution. And while he criticized decisions of the courts which is the democratic process available to every American, then as now, no act or word of his can be found on the pages of history which gives any support to the argument that because he disagreed with the Court he would have attempted to pack it with "King's men," and thus overrule its previous judgment. He would not and did not at any time thus attempt to destroy the checks and balances of the Constitution.

It is interesting also to note that his court criticisms, like those of Lincoln with respect to the Dred Scott decision, were criticisms of the trend of court judgments to give the Federal government *more power*, rather than as recently, decisions which have asserted *limits* upon that power in favor of the states. The trend of decisions of the Supreme Court today which have been subject to such strong criticism, is the direct opposite of the trend of decisions of the court to which Jefferson found exception. The same may be said of Abraham Lincoln. What he found wrong with the Dred Scott case was the assertion of Federal power with respect to the sovereignty of a state. Illinois was a free state. Dred Scott as a negro slave was voluntarily taken by his master into Illinois. It was the contention of Lincoln that when that slave breathed free air, under the law of Illinois, he became a free man.

The historic disagreements of Jefferson and Lincoln with

decisions of the United States Supreme Court were that those decisions, in their judgment, were unduly extending Federal power over matters which they felt were more properly committed to the sovereignty of the states.

Jefferson's experience with the Alien and Sedition laws under Adams' administration would never have led Jefferson in this 20th century to have advocated a law which would have permitted some court official in the city of Washington to assign Federal judges to rove around throughout all of the Federal districts and there sit in special cases for the purpose of obtaining convictions of American citizens which the Federal government might be doubtful of obtaining if the resident judge in that district were to try the case.

But this was a part of the court packing plan and fully as dangerous to the rights of the American citizen as the effort to pack the Supreme Court even though the latter was for the express purpose, as admitted by Senator Logan of Kentucky who had charge of the bill on the floor of the Senate, to obtain a reversal of important decisions of the court.

Jefferson advocated going to the people on the question as to whether the Federal government should have more power. He did not believe that Congress and the President should assume a power and then create a rubber stamp court to confirm the assumption. It is plain that if this is to become the prevailing philosophy in America, constitutional government as we have known it has "gone with the wind." We will then have government vacillating with each election.

All long range business planning would then be forced to guess what a future majority of Congress or the future whim of a president would command them to do and with what result? The same result that Jefferson said would happen,

> "changes of majorities will be changing the system backwards and forwards *so that no undertaking under it will be safe.*"

The growth of this country has depended in large part upon the fact that we have constitutional government and not strictly speaking majority government. The Constitution has given stability and continuity with resulting confidence in the planning of the business enterprise of this nation;—the laying out of our railroads and the building up of our industries which in the ordinary course cannot hope to amortize their original investment for years to come. Under the Constitution, however, men have felt safe to buy the 10, 20, 30, 40, 50-year bonds of American transportation and industry knowing that as long as the Constitution stands and as long as an independent judiciary stands to hold the majority within constitutional limits, their investments will be safe against legislative confiscation.

Jefferson did bitterly criticize the decision in Marbury v. Madison pronounced in 1803 by Chief Justice Marshall, his kinsman. This decision for the first time declared an act of Congress unconstitutional. Jefferson disagreed with some of the views expressed in that opinion but he continued as president from the date of its rendition in 1803, with party majorities in both the House and the Senate, for six years longer until March 4, 1809. With all this power in his hands he never suggested packing the Supreme Court of John Marshall for the purpose of overthrowing this decision.

As stated, Jefferson would grant all necessary power to the central government. But he would do so openly by amending the Constitution. He would thus preserve constitutional morality.

Today it may be necessary for the Federal government to have more power. If so, let the question be submitted to the people in accordance with the Constitution. The present administration has submitted not a single amendment to the people except to repeal prohibition and so legalize the sale of intoxicating liquors. It has feared to let the people pass on far-reaching proposals to change their government.

The Reorganization Bill is the other great issue raised in the

75th Congress. No one can understand that bill as originally prepared unless he understands the Humphreys case. Mr. Humphreys was a member of the Federal Trade Commission. The law creating that commission was enacted in President Wilson's time. It provided that members of the commission might be removed only for specified acts such as inefficiency or malfeasance in office. In 1933 President Roosevelt removed Mr. Humphreys, a member of the commission, not for any of the causes assigned in the statute but for the sole reason as stated that "your mind and my mind do not go along together" on questions of policy.

The Supreme Court of the United States on the same day it handed down the N.R.A. decision, unanimously, conservatives and liberals, held that the act of President Roosevelt in removing Mr. Humphreys was an unconstitutional exercise of executive power.

The Executive Reorganization Bill as proposed by the President's Committee in January and February 1937 would have given the President all the power which the Supreme Court said he did not possess in the Humphreys case. It would have given him and his successors the power to remove any member or all members of any of the great government commissions at any time, for any reason or no reason. It would have given him the power to abolish the commission itself and transfer and re-transfer its powers in whole or in part to some other agency or some other man, or group of men, whom the president might select, who need not even run the gauntlet of ratification in the United States Senate.

This bill would have given the President and his successors complete control over the decisions, policies, acts and judgments of the Interstate Commerce Commission, the Federal Trade Commission, the Securities and Exchange Commission, the National Labor Relations Board, and all the other great quasi-legislative and quasi-judicial bodies established by Congress. It would have destroyed the only independent check on the expenditure of billions of public money. In so doing it would have gathered into one man's hands more power than has ever been concentrated in America. This is more power than a good man should want or a bad man should have.

How does all this stand up against Jefferson's declaration—

"I am not for transferring the powers of the states to the General Government and of those of that government to the executive branch."

also—

"The way to have good government is not to trust it all to one."

CHAPTER 17

"BUCCANEERS OF BUSINESS"

Business men with high blood pressure should skip this chapter. They will not like it. And it might prove fatal.

Others, however, may recall the old adage "faithful are the wounds of a friend." With smelling salts on hand they may venture to proceed.

If in the perhaps not distant future free enterprise—and with it free government—should vanish from American life, an inquest is certain to be held. On that day, one of the saddest in history, many witnesses will be called. The question, who killed Cock Robin or permitted him to die, will receive many answers. Some will blame Moscow; others, Tugwell; others, the failure to require the teacher's oath in the public schools; others, the failure to deport the Communists, or to shout loudly enough "down with the reds"; still others, the vain but reckless pretensions of pulpit politicians "most ignorant of what they are most assured."

All these may influence the verdict, but I believe the final judgment of the impartial historian will be that free enterprise died in the house of its friends, its death wound given by its beneficiaries, not by its foes.

In my book, "Hot Oil," I said:

"Can business men run business in the interest of the whole people? Can profits be harmonized with the needs of the nation for today and for tomorrow? Must the states surrender their historic jurisdiction to the nation? In a word, can we secure social objectives without regimentation, prosperity without paternalism? Or, turning the question around, will paternalism produce prosperity? How much of liberty can we afford to pay for the 'promise' of

133

security? Or will bureaucracy, in destroying liberty, also destroy the efficiency in the production and distribution of wealth which alone makes security possible?

"If democracy fails, as so many in these difficult days seem even anxious to predict, it will be because it fails to meet the new problems of a new industrial world in which economic structures transcend state lines.

"What, then, is the true boundary between business and government, the states and the nation, individual responsibility and public control, the line 'which shall combine that degree of liberty without which law is tyranny, with that degree of law without which liberty becomes license'?

"What are the proper limits of the functions and agencies of government? Those limits will be extended only as the failures of industry make the extension seem imperative. If business proves incapable of self-discipline in the interest of the millions, government will occupy new ground. The millions will demand it, and they have the votes. They will fly 'to ills they know not of' rather than continue to embrace conditions that have become intolerable. No constitution, however revered and hallowed with the blood of the fathers, will long check their course.

"The fate of America is still in the hands of those who have the greatest stake in America—the leaders of enterprise and their shareholders. Will they, who have the most to lose, do most to serve?"

Let us be honest with ourselves and with the truth. Without entering now upon the merits or demerits of N.R.A. or A.A.A., or the Potato Bill or other similar legislation, where did these bills find their origin? First, in the breakdown of capitalism and, second, at the urging of capitalists.

Take N.R.A. I was present at its birth. I was in the Ways and Means Committee room when a representative, not of Karl Marx, but of American business, the president of the United States Chamber of Commerce, urged that legislation upon the Congress of the United States in behalf of the business interests of the country—a fact eloquently corroborated by Mr. W. T. Holliday in his testimony before the Cole Committee.

Take A.A.A. Whence came the demand for and ready acquiescence in "regimentation" by the most individualistic and sturdy of all members of the capitalist class—the American farmer? What apparent necessity induced him to reverse the habits of centuries, to kill pigs before they matured, and to plow under cotton and wheat before it was ripe for the harvest? It was because the loss of foreign markets has caused unsaleable surpluses to accumulate. And why did farm markets disappear? It was, in part at least, due to tariffs lobbied for by American capitalists which in turn provoked reprisals abroad, and thus farm surpluses and crop control and "regimentation" at home. For a decade American industry, in power at Washington, saw the free enterprise of farming slowly starve to the point of desperation.

If in the future there shall be a struggle for power in this country between the classes, industry would do well to have on its side the 30,000,000 Americans who live on the farms and in the county-seat towns and villages of America. The "farm problem" is the problem of industry also.

When it is said that free enterprise has failed, my answer is that we have not permitted it to work. We have impeded it with a tanglefoot of our own making.

Despite all this sudden talk of a "planned economy," the fact is that we have never had a wholly free economy in this country. A policy of protective tariffs, for example, is in itself a repeal of the law of supply and demand.

Everywhere we see business men seeking to sustain themselves and their prices by "controlling the market," by monopoly, by subsidies, by franchises, by licenses, by certificates of public interest and necessity, by patents, by trademarks, by "pegging the dollar" to sustain credits, by devaluation to obtain advantages in international trade, by cheapening the dollar to pay debts through rising prices, by shifting the tax load to their competitors, by statutory price fixing, by retail-sales control; in other words, by "regimentation"—for the other fellow.

The protest against this sort of thing was, in my judgment, the highlight of the 1936 campaign.

In a notable paper four years ago Gustav Cassel of Sweden pointed out that the pressure of business interests upon government for special privileges for themselves or legislative handcuffs for their competitors leads inevitably to "planned economy" and, hence, to dictatorship.

No government can write tariffs, license importers and exporters, pay subsidies, impose quotas, increase production, restrict production, regulate rates of foreign exchange, secretly manipulate huge stabilization funds, enter upon competitive under-valuation of national currencies, extend or restrict credit, raise and lower interest rates, fix prices, issue embargoes, regulate division of earnings between spending and investment, etc., without making mistakes which require corrections leading to more mistakes, without calling forth claims for compensating measures, in the same way that tariffs for manufacturers led to the demand for a "farmer's tariff" or its equivalent; or, more recently, when the control of cotton production led to tobacco control, and from tobacco to peanuts to potatoes. Similarly, government-financed hydroelectric power plants, which compete with coal, increase the demand for subsidies for coal mines and for restriction of production.

Because government grants favors to capitalists, it is appealed to to grant equalizing favors to workers.

Because it creates agencies to benefit producers, it perforce must create other agencies to protect consumers—the consumers' bureau and the producers' bureau, each begging Congress for more money to checkmate the other!

And so government goes about grasping for more and more power to cope with the abuse of the privileges it has itself created.

If it be said: "Upon what meat doth this, our Cæsar, feed that he has grown so great?" the answer must be that the pressure of business interests forced the meat down the great man's throat.

Meantime, the invisible government is constantly at work behind the scenes to hog the cake and distribute the crusts of governmental favor. And all of this, let me repeat, is initiated not by pink young professors, but by business interests seeking statutory refuges from the competitive struggle they praise so highly—on paper.

Meantime, members of legislative bodies are overworked with problems beyond their time, strength, and experience, and outside their proper jurisdiction. The inevitable tendency is to delegate their powers to a vast bureaucracy. What they themselves do is done poorly, and the resulting loss of confidence in the ability as well as the disinterestedness of parliamentary government calls for louder cries for stronger men, and hence for the Strong Man himself, who in turn makes his mistakes—of whom Napoleon and the Kaiser are only two of many that sent whole nations to disaster.

It cannot be denied that the same government that fixes prices for commodities, rents, and interest can with equal logic fix wages, either up or down, and shorten or lengthen hours of work. It all depends on who controls the government. In Germany and other countries today industrial workers are reported to be required to carry a "work card," which easily becomes the European equivalent of the hated black list. Take it or leave it! Is this to be the reward of the American workman for rushing to Washington for the solution of his troubles? If so, "planned economy" will have a sour taste for his children.

In their international aspect this Chinese maze of trade restrictions might as well be recognized for what it is—the economic and monetary equivalent of war, with Armageddon only a step away.

The future of free enterprise goes far deeper than "is dreamed of in our philosophy." It not only involves the future of free government, but the future of civilization—any kind of civilization.

It is one thing when business competes on its own hook for international markets. But when government itself becomes the active partner of business men in throttling their international competitors, the latter rush to their governments to make political and military answers to economic arguments.

Thus the struggle is broadened and intensified. Is not the whole effort for national security rapidly increasing national insecurity? And is not every supposed trade gain offset a thousand times by the weight of armament and the cost of war—actual and potential? The world, it seems, can have trade and peace—or trade stoppage and war.

Coming nearer home, what bill in recent years had more of the essence of collectivism, the destruction of states' rights, the regimentation of enterprise, than the Thomas-Disney Bill which would, if enacted, give an official at Washington the power to fix the daily production of petroleum from every well in America and therefore, indirectly, the income of the owner and the price paid by the buyer.

Again, without discussing the merits or necessity of the bill, it is the simple truth that it was the representatives of the industry itself who rushed to Washington crying, "O beneficent bureaucrats, uncontaminated as you are with any knowledge of the problem of petroleum, and with that high detachment and objective viewpoint—resulting from never having seen an oil well—save us ere we perish, save us from ourselves!"

From my conning tower at Washington I saw another great industry, not rushing to the Capitol, but dragged there to stand trial for its own misdeeds. I heard the astonishing story of a dark jungle of holding companies pyramided 10 stories high upon each other—the hiding place of financial freebooters. I saw the leaders of that industry, with ashen faces, unable to defend themselves. Some were personally vulnerable, and those who were not felt forced by a spurious fraternalism to keep the door shut upon the skeletons in the closets of their industry rather than clean house. I said to some of these men that it passed my understanding how they could do such a marvelous job on their physical plants and equipment—a miracle of science—and be so utterly dumb and deaf and blind on their public relations. I said to them: "What you need is a Kenesaw Mountain Landis, a czar of your own choosing, whose sole function shall be to call foul balls, and whose contract shall expire the instant he ever says 'strike one.'"

I heard the story of stock split-ups, the watering of capital structures, the sale in interstate commerce of worthless Peruvian and European bonds and domestic stocks, in which $25,-000,000,000 of the savings of thrift and toil were lost beyond recall, and my committee wrote the securities act of 1933.

Industrial self-discipline! I saw the stock exchanges and banks finance the bubble of speculation until it finally burst in ruin in 1929 with a shrinkage in values of stocks and bonds alone—to say nothing of commodities and real estate, rural and urban—of $91,729,000,000, or three times the amount of the World War debt. And then, with little help and much opposition, my committee wrote the stock-exchange act of 1934.

Industrial self-discipline! In times called prosperous I saw 11,000 banks, nearly a third of the nation's total, close their doors with $5,000,000,000 of hard-won savings dissipated to the four winds of heaven, and under the very Dome of the Nation's Capitol I heard an old man say: "To hell with the Constitution. It did not save my savings."

Industrial self-discipline! A few years earlier I saw the legitimate wine, beer, and liquor industry—through illegitimate practices winked at by themselves—write their own ticket to exile and heard them pronounce the death sentence on their own hundreds of millions of investment.

In 1933 I spent a year as a member of a House committee

on government competition with private enterprise. We developed the facts. We showed socialism coming through the back door, but except their own ox was gored we got practically no support from either business men or political leaders.

I pick up the Statistical Abstract of the United States, and read that, in 1928, 511 men had net taxable realized incomes of a million dollars or more, averaging $2,270,000 each, or $7,000 a day apiece, and totalling altogether $1,108,862,000—only 2 per cent of which, let it be noted, represented compensation for services actually rendered—a total *net* income to 511 men greater than the *gross* income of all the wheat and cotton farmers of the nation, aggregating, with wives and children, some 10,000,000 Americans.

> "Ill fares the land, to hastening ills a prey
> Where wealth accumulates, and men decay."

And then, a little later, I saw this capitalistic system collapse, stabbed in the house of its friends, its blood sucked by its beneficiaries, and 15,000,000 idle men dependent upon private charity or public dole—an army which, placed in single column two feet apart, would reach across the continent and *back*—America's question mark to free enterprise.

Everything that is wrong in this picture is wrong because it is a violation of Jeffersonian philosophy. "Equal rights for all, special privileges for none." And that is the economic and political phrasing of the Golden Rule which is never violated by man, or men, without penalties which a just God inexorably exacts because He *is* just.

The great enemy of business, as well as of government, and democracy, is Privilege.

CHAPTER 18

STATESMEN IN INDUSTRY

"Gentlemen of Industry, we in this room are responsible for the welfare of millions of our fellow citizens, their wives, their children. We are citizens of the most blest nation on earth, endowed as is no other, . . . Is this program of industry fair, social, constructive, liberal? If it is not we are prepared to make it so."

—Colby M. Chester.

In this tanglefoot that is throttling and discrediting our constitutional government, states' rights, free enterprise, and the dignity of the individual, there is an imperative and bitter need for new Jeffersons and Twentieth Century Lincolns who will free business men from the shackles wrought by themselves.

I ask one intensely serious question: If the leaders and owners of the American system are too lazy to wash their dirty dishes, too selfish to be intelligent, and too timid to stick their necks out in defense of free enterprise and constitutional government, who will defend it?

I see business men economize down to the last two inches of the lead pencils of their clerks, and themselves sweat and slave for twenty or thirty years to achieve a competency for the evening of life; and then, when the periodic crash comes, but with youth behind them, and the old push and drive no longer theirs, I see them with sublime courage start to weave anew the pattern of their hopes, but apparently with no thought whatever to softening the downward curve of the next collapse, or to the survival of the system itself to which they have given all their strength.

I have no wish to be unjust. The average business man is so engrossed with the daily task, so harassed with making out reports to government bureaucrats, that he has to keep his nose to the grindstone from dawn to dark. As an individual, he is practically helpless. But it does seem that trade associations generally, as well as many of the larger companies, could well afford to have on their boards a man whose sole responsibility is public relations in the broadest sense, a man of unimpeachable integrity, to act as a tribune for the people, whose constant care it shall be that the priceless ingredient of character and fair dealing with worker and customer and government shall be woven into the fabric of free enterprise. Such a man would not alone sell his industry to the public, but would be equally diligent to sell the public to his industry.

And then, to pursue the idea further, suppose the public-relations members of each of the five hundred and more existing trade associations (and you are to imagine them as containing men of the standing and character of former President Eliot of Harvard, or Justice Hughes of the United States Supreme Court) were to organize, informally, a Supreme Council of American Enterprise, with sufficient funds to conduct inquiries and report from time to time on "the state of the Union." Let me *italicize* the word *"Union."*

Certainly it is becoming plain that the profession of public relations requires experience and training as specialized as that of sales manager or of laboratory technician.

Perhaps this suggestion is wholly impracticable; but, as I reconnoiter the field, it seems desirable, if not imperative, that some means be found to mobilize the conscience and enlightened self-interest—not of one division alone, but of the entire army of American industry, business, agriculture and finance. Such a mobilization would be both for offense and defense. It would be the sharp critic and ruthless surgeon of evil practices on the one hand, and on the other the stout champion of the American system, minus its crooks and its hogs.

There are those who will sneer at what they would call my naive assumption that there is a conscience in American business, and will use against me the articles of indictment drawn in the previous chapter.

I know better. I know the average business man is just as anxious to deal justly with his men and with the public as the average politician. I would rather have the judgment and conscience of the man who is close to his men and the public than the *ipse dixit* of the intelligentsia who would rule the universe from their garrets or their thrones.

The fault, or rather failure, of business executives, is not that they are soulless and selfish, but rather that they are, or have been too preoccupied with the daily problems of their business. It may be due also, in part, to the fact (as one of the major executives of industry informs me) that so many of the top men and members of executive committees have spent their previous years as specialists in a single branch of their industries and have never been under the necessity "to see life steadily and to see it whole."

But all this only explains, yet does not refute, my contention that industry's greatest weakness today is in its public relations.

Let me return to what I was saying about conscience in business.

On Constitution Day in September 1936 I addressed the Daughters of the American Revolution. I recounted this story, and it is a true story. The editor of a fine little newspaper in Indiana told me how he went through the depression. When advertising and subscribers fell off, he called in his men, sixty in number, from the oldest pressman to the youngest cub reporter. He said to them, "Boys, we have got to retrench to keep this paper alive. But we will all go up or down together. This paper is in the red, but I do not intend any one of you to see red. I will show my good faith by taking the biggest cut, both in dollars and per cent." They faced the music together.

Not a man deserted the paper, and the paper did not desert a man. The editor said to me, "If St. Peter ever pins any medal on my bosom, it will be because all through the depression every man in my employ found something in his pay envelope every Saturday."

And I said to the D.A.R.'s., "That man did more to save the Constitution than all the editorials he might have written in its honor and glory after he had fired half his men."

There are thousands of such men who made similar sacrifices to keep their men employed, and who equally "deserve well of the Republic." Others had the desire to do so, but were forced to shut down by circumstances beyond their control. I am ready to go to bat for that kind of business man.

But, unfortunately, there are many others who retrenched only in pay rolls, dumping their workers out on the streets to be taken care of by relief agencies—and who now beef about the public debt incurred in keeping their former workers from starving.

It is a harsh thing to say—as harsh and as kind and as kindly meant as the surgeon who tells you an operation is imperative— but is it not the cold fact that business men generally have lost the confidence of their own workers? Is it not the fact that the business man and the politician have been competing for the good will of the worker, and the business man has lost? Why? Maybe it is not his fault. Maybe it is due to forces beyond his control—the war, the depression—but I think we would be more sure of the survival of free enterprise if we stopped looking for alibis and said, "Well, some of it is my fault, and all of it is my job."

Where did business men get in the fall of 1936 with their attack on the social security act? They got the Bronx cheer! That attack was the supreme blunder of the Republican campaign. The workers refused to believe that their employers wanted to improve an admittedly imperfect law. They were convinced that the attack was on the principle of the law itself.

How wrong were they? No answer, perhaps, can be given. But certainly the principle of "avoiding the appearance of evil" was so clearly indicated that I am surprised that persons who call themselves astute began throwing boomerangs so viciously— at themselves!

To wait until a law has been on the statute books for four-teen months before suddenly notifying workers how terrible it is, was in itself an open advertisement that shoddy goods were being sold.

An objective viewpoint would have avoided a blunder like that. That is why free enterprise needs a lot of Judge Landises of public relations. Many sincere business men, busy as they are in the squirrel cage where losses constantly chase profits, had never even heard of the social security act. But that again proves the very point I am trying to make—the need for a division of enterprise marked "industrial statesmanship."

Consider, as one among many, the problem of old age in this machine civilization of modern city life. The most amaz-ing change in population trends is going on before our very eyes. There were 34 per cent more people over 65 in 1930 than in 1910—only 20 years earlier. That proportion in the upper age levels is almost certain to increase. In fact, actuaries for great life insurance companies predict that by 1970—only 32 years from now—there will be more people over 50 than under 20; in other words, that the problem of the average man only a few years hence will be to take care of his parents rather than his children—the greatest shift in age groupings, probably, since the world began. It is due, of course, to two main factors: Fewer babies born per 1000 of population; but of those which are born, because of the marvelous conquests of medicine— principally in the diseases of childbood, youth and young man-hood—more live into the upper age levels.

But as your average line moves up, the industrial deadline

moves down. The two lines cross, and the point of their cross-ing marks one of the battlefields where free enterprise and free government are to be saved—if they are to be saved. For when the age line passes the industrial deadline, there is little point left in the sound old slogans of "rugged individualism" or "initiative" or "courage." These old virtues have lost their meaning. The door to the "land of opportunity" in which these virtues can long live and thrive has then been closed.

Combine all this with the passing of the free land of the West, the recurrence of "boom and bust," of depressions which wipe out banks and other institutions where the savings of thrift and toil are invested, and, last, that other great shift to city life from rural life where, as in the "good old days" there were always useful chores for grandma and grandpa to do, and you have the challenge of Dr. Townsend, a challenge that can-not be laughed off.

When I speak of industrial statesmanship, it is problems like this I have in mind. What are the leaders of our enterprise going to do about them?

If they do nothing—or little that is effective—free enter-prise, in the years just ahead, is going to be subjected to a con-stantly increasing and irresistible pressure from these oppor-tunity-less groups to have the politicians take over the manage-ment, if not the ownership, of your business—for their benefit.

Take unemployment. In terms of social ethics, where does the dollar derive a claim to being paid dividends during periods of depression, superior to the claims of the laid-off worker to being paid unemployment reserves? Why are reserves justified for depreciation, depletion, and amortization of machinery and plant, and reserves not justified for "human obsolescence"?

These are not the questions of a long-haired radical or soap-box orator. I quote the exact language of Charles Evans Hughes, Chief Justice of the United States Supreme Court, who wrote the minority opinion in the railroad pension case:

"What sound distinction, from a constitutional viewpoint, is there between compelling reasonable compensation for those *injured* without any fault of the employer (as in workmen's compensation acts) and requiring a fair allowance for those who practically give their lives to the service and are incapacitated by the wear and tear of time, the attrition of the years? I can perceive no constitutional ground upon which the one can be upheld and the other condemned. The fundamental consideration which supports this type of legislation is that *industry should take care of its human wastage,* whether that is due to accident or age."

American industry has been built on the struggle for the consumer's dollar by offering most and best for least. That is competitive capitalism at its best. It becomes destructive when it is a competition of who will pay the least wages. The responsibility of industrial management to build a floor below which wages are not to go is tremendous. American industries must cooperate with each other, and with government, to find ways and means by which the masses who wish to work may live in decent comfort and security. The choice, as I see it, is between wages and taxes; between a self-disciplined and humanized capitalism and state socialism; between free government based on the consent of the governed and ancient tyrannies under modern masks.

Although I cannot demonstrate it on a blackboard, I have a feeling—as compelling as a religious conviction—that if industry will constantly pass on to the worker and the customer the savings of labor-saving machinery and invention, rather than siphon them off into the pools of watered securities, as was too much done before the crash, it will by that process keep distribution and production in balance, and go as far toward Utopia as our poor human natures will go or be driven.

To accomplish this tools may be necessary. But the spirit must come first, and it is my hope that it will be supplied in gratifying measure by the leaders of industry themselves. What is desperately needed right now is the *spirit* and the *will* for fair dealing between capital and labor, labor and labor, industry and government.

With this, plus our technology, invention and power, nothing is impossible. Without it anything is possible. Yes, anything—*it can happen here!!*

We must be cold sober about this question. If looking from our windows we saw nothing but the Jamestown of 1607, or the Plymouth Rock of 1620, the wilderness, forests to clear, stumps to pull, quagmire roads, whale oil lights, greased paper windows, poor tools, poor seed, sour soil, the power of oxen and human backs, distant markets—we would accept, and thankfully, as our forefathers did, the meager fruits of our toil. Our fathers never saw *poverty* in the midst of *plenty*. But what they saw is not what we see. Dr. Virgil Jordan is dead right about this. The millions of our people, the masses, if you please, see science, technology, power; they see the forces of nature harnessed to the service of man; they see a thousand, a million horsepower where Captain John Smith or William Bradford saw a single horse; and they cannot understand and will not accept the Twentieth Century paradox of poverty in the midst of potential plenty. "Bread lines standing knee deep in wheat," present a question which they think, and think rightly, our statesmen in government and our statesmen in labor and industry must solve.

There has been much political unfairness toward business and business men in recent years. We live in a profit and *loss* economy. That economy cannot guarantee profits or plenty in and of itself. If wealth is to be distributed, it must first be produced. In the long run each must earn his daily bread. There is no cornucopia anywhere. There is no panacea anywhere. There is no political patent medicine to cure our ills. Government, through taxation, may take from one and give to the other. But this is simply a transfer of wealth from one pocket to another. It adds nothing to the total amount of wealth, the total purchasing power of our people.

This is no time for demagogues and rabble-rousers. This is no time for the sowers of the seeds of class hatred. "Every man a king" is as false as it is dangerous. Except to attempt to prevent their being exploited, no system of government, no set of politicians, can do very much for the drunkards, the shiftless, the ne'er-do-wells, the gullible buyers of gold bricks. In the times of the Old Testament it was noted that the "vines of the drunken husbandman are choked with weeds."

But those, who by honest toil, thrift, sobriety, sacrifice, careful living, or by inventive and business genius, have earned and saved a few thousand dollars, or a million dollars, with which they have built factories or which they have loaned to those who need it, do not deserve to be held up to contempt as "princes of privilege." I am not speaking of the buccaneers of business. I am speaking of those who have accumulated something as a reward of useful work by hand or brain. On the other hand, we gain nothing by describing everybody with holes in his shoes as a sort of civic hero who should be permanently pensioned as an underprivileged patriot.

A political leader who promises to tax the worker to enrich the shirker, to plunder savings to give to the shiftless, is no better than a poisoner of wells.

Our program must be for those who *want to work*. It is the responsibility of our generation to reopen and keep open the doors of opportunity which former generations of immigrants found here in America from the days of Plymouth Rock. Our duty it is to remember that the end of the American frontier has created problems which did not exist while that great safety valve was working for the benefit of our teeming millions.

Our responsibility it is to recognize the plight and solve the problems of those whom age has carried beyond the industrial deadline. How can we harness for the millions the benefits of technology, the economies of mass production, the rewards of invention and the sorceries of science, to the political stability of the New England Town Meeting and the economic security, the unhurried pace, and the sense of peace in the little villages and county seat towns in "Happy Valley"?

Can we regain freedom and the opportunity which freedom gives, not as a primitive right in the wilderness, but as a civilized achievement? We must believe that we can. We must believe that our situation is not hopeless, that our fate will not be the bread and circuses of modern Caesars; that a WPA future is not all that awaits our children.

We have sought in the wrong direction the solutions of these problems. We must reverse our course. We must move as Jefferson would towards *diversification and decentralization* political, economic, industrial, and financial.

We must revitalize democracy at the rim to prevent its rotting at the center. We must send sap to the leaf in order to preserve life in the trunk. We must recognize centralization for what it is in truth—a reactionary movement, a Tory philosophy, and the negation of democracy. This is the problem and this is the opportunity for Statesmen in Industry, and Statesmen in Labor, to solve by common counsel.

CHAPTER 19

ALTERNATIVES TO EMPIRE

"Why should not the powers that are reserved to the states'
sovereignty be exercised by these sovereignties under a firm
resolve to make it wholly unnecessary that this continued
pressure to force the national government into the performance of the duties they ought to perform should continue?"
—Elihu Root.

Where is the true boundary between business and government, the states and the nation, individual and corporate responsibility and public welfare and control—the line which shall
combine "that degree of liberty without which law is tyranny,
and that degree of law without which liberty is license"?

No Jeffersonian denies that in certain fields the Federal government is alone fitted to act effectively. Elsewhere, as an illustration, mention has been made of the Federal control of radio
communications.

It is, however, emphatically not true in the majority of instances and from the necessities of the case that the Federal
government must act because the separate state cannot alone act
effectively. If we are not to turn this union of states into a
bureaucratic empire, with all of the dangers to democracy implied in that program, we should solve outside of Washington
all problems with respect to which the states individually and
collectively may act *with effect*. Thus we shall retain the direction of local and regional matters in the hands of those most
directly concerned. Thus we shall also retain the benefits, and
they have been very great, of our dual form of government—

the ancient balance between freedom and power, liberty and law, stability and growth.

In our fathers' time this balance was struck between nation and state, county and hamlet and their citizens along political and geographical boundaries. Now that economic structures transcend state lines, controls must be developed commensurate with the necessity of causing these economic structures to function to the public interest.

It must be recognized that a feeling of public helplessness has developed with respect to the ever widening circle of Federal control. This helplessness, however, is not warranted. There are effective controls outside of Federal control for many very important functions of government and industry. The trend toward centralized government is not a matter of inescapable necessity. It has gone on purely by default of local and state authority on the one hand, and on the other the nationalistic views and ambitions which have mushroomed at Washington.

What are some of these alternatives to empire? Among others, let us mention uniform state laws, reciprocal state legislation, and interstate compacts. All of these controls are available without changing or straining the Constitution, and without placing in the hands of a single government control over all the activities of American life. It is only when, after a fair and candid trial of these alternative controls, and a resulting conclusion that they cannot be exercised effectively in some particular case, that we should then go to Washington for legislative relief.

If the president, any president, with the tremendous prestige of his office and with the White House as his sounding board, were to urge these alternative controls in place of Federal control, we would find, I am convinced, that a major part of the present trend toward centralization would be wholly obviated. It is a great tragedy that in recent years we have not had a president who has sought to find and to urge others to find solutions back home in the state, and among the states, and thus prevent the concentration of all public responsibility at the nation's capital.

Let us review some of these alternatives. As an example, take the legal instruments under which practically all of the enormous volume of the nation's business is done; promissory notes, bills of exchange, acceptances, sales contracts, warehouse receipts, etc. Obviously it is useful, in fact often indispensable, that the law with respect to these instruments be uniform among the states. That has been accomplished without changing the Constitution of the United States, without centering any authority at Washington, without an act of Congress.

This work began as far back at 1889. The American Bar Association appointed a special committee to draft and submit to the various states uniform state laws. As a result we have today many uniform acts governing these instruments by which the enormous business of the nation is conducted. The Negotiable Instruments Act is now in force in every jurisdiction in the United States. The law is the same in every state of the union with very minor variations and, as stated, it has all been accomplished without rushing to Washington. Nevertheless any state which, in the wisdom of its own legislature, considers its situation sufficiently different from the situation of other states is left free, if it chooses, to change its own law to accommodate the convenience of its own citizens. Because it seems desirable that the public should be encouraged as much as possible against this trend toward centralization of power, I append a list of 32 uniform Acts which have been adopted in ten or more states. In addition, the National Conference of Commissioners on Uniform State Laws have drawn up 33 other Acts which have been adopted in less than 10 states, and are now pending action by other state legislatures.

Those which have been adopted in more than 10 states, with the number of states adopting them are:—

*Adopted by
Number of
States*

Act to Secure the Attendance of Witnesses from
    without the State in Criminal Cases 18
Aeronautics Act 22
Bills of Lading Act 29
Conditional Sales Act 10
Criminal Extradition Act 15
Criminal Extradition Act as Revised 10
Declaratory Judgments Act 25
Desertion and Non-Support Act 20
Extradition of Persons of Unsound Mind Act . . . 11
Federal Tax Lien Registration Act 19
Fiduciaries Act 17
Firearms Act 11
Flag Act 10
Foreign Depositions Act 11
Fraudulent Conveyance Act 16
Limited Partnership Act 21
Narcotic Drug Act 36
Negotiable Instruments Act 53
Partnership Act 19
Proof of Statutes Act 25
Reciprocal Transfer Tax Act 17
Sales Act 36
    Amendments to same 10
Stock Transfer Act 26
Motor Vehicle Registration Act 10
Operators' and Chauffeurs' License 14
Motor Vehicle Anti-Theft Act 10
Regulating Traffic on Highways 19
Veterans' Guardianship Act 33
Warehouse Receipts Act 48
Amendments to Warehouse Receipts Act 14
Execution of Foreign Wills 11

No one can read this impressive list of instances in which the states by common action have adopted uniform legislation, and consider, also the 30-odd other acts which have been adopted thus far by less than ten states, without becoming convinced that here is an important method for the states to take common action which has proved highly serviceable. Many of these acts are of very great importance, many, in fact, are far more important than most legislation passed by Congress.

There are other organizations doing effective work along similar lines. One is the Council of State Governments. Thirty-six states so far have set up permanent interstate co-operative commissions. In 1935, these interstate commissioners met with professors from 26 of the leading law schools and drew up a four-point program:

One was a statute giving officers in "fresh pursuit" of a criminal the authority to cross state lines and make arrests in the other state into which the criminal had fled. Twenty-two states adopted that law within two years.

A second statute deals with the extradition of criminals and so far has been adopted by 18 states.

A third is a statute with reference to the reciprocal supervision of paroled convicts;—adopted by 21 states.

A fourth is a statute with reference to the attendance of material out-of-the-state witnesses; adopted by 22 states. This makes it possible in a lawsuit to require the attendance of a witness even though he lives outside the state in which the case is being tried.

In view of the fact that the crime problem is a very great one, it is gratifying to see that in the past two or three years, the states have been accepting their own responsibilities and making it as easy for the state law to reach across a state line as for the criminal.

Contrast this with the views expressed by President Roosevelt at Chicago, in October 1936. He said—

"America is an economic unit. New modern methods of transportation and communication have made us economically as well as politically a single nation. Because kidnappers and bank robbers could in a high-powered car safely

cross state lines it became necessary in order to protect our
people, to invoke the power of Federal government. . . .
There was no power under heaven that could protect the
people against this sort of thing except the people's government at Washington."

On the contrary, the Federal government is not the only
"power under heaven" capable of dealing with problems of interstate crime. The Federal government may properly supple-
ment but not supplant the state governments. For example
there is the Lindbergh Law, making it a Federal offense to transport a kidnapped child across a state line, legislation which I
voted for. For the purpose of this argument it is only necessary
to point out the actual record of performance being made by
the states. It contrasts effectively with the crime record being
made by the Federal government in its own home in Washington, D. C., as set forth in another chapter.

Other matters upon which the Council for State Governments is at work deals with such modern problems as the trailer,
schooling for trailer children, taxation of trailers, safety requirements with respect to them, uniform sanitary codes for trailer
camps, uniform legislation covering the migration of persons
on relief and regulating the question of their domicile—so far
adopted by nine states—legislation with respect to the inspection of motor vehicles, their brakes, headlights, etc. in the interest of safety to the public. It is work along these lines that has
been described by the distinguished historian, James Truslow
Adams, as—

> ". . . the only way of preserving democratic institutions.
> No work being done today in America is of more vital
> importance than that being done for state cooperation. The
> public does not hear much of those but it should hear
> more."

But we have not yet exhausted these "alternatives to Federal
empire." The question of interstate rivers necessarily concerns

the people living in more than one state involving as it does the use of water for reclamation, irrigation, the purity of water for water supply, the dumping of sewage, requiring industrial plants to treat their own wastes, together with the allied problems of power, flood control, etc. Under the sponsorship of the Council of State Governments, as an example, Delaware, New Jersey, Pennsylvania and New York have set up the Interstate Commission on the Delaware River, for the purpose of solving these interstate waterway problems without passing the buck to Washington. It will interest many to know that this Council is erecting in the city of Chicago an interstate building to house its activities—a sort of League of Nations' palace for the American States, a capitol for cooperation, not compulsion. As has been said, "It has been easier for the United States to negotiate with Siam than for two adjoining states to reach an agreement, just because there was no permanent machinery for such negotiations."

The idea that the states are helpless to solve problems requiring the action of more than one state individually, is just one of these readymade mass production synthetic dogmas which we, a nation of headline readers, swallow whole. Its dam is lazy thinking and its sire "passing the buck." It was conceived in carelessness, born in complacency, and reared in cowardice.

But from the facts recited above, we have the answer to the belief, apparently entertained by President Roosevelt, that the *only* alternative to Federal jurisdiction over all these matters is intolerable chaos.

Nowhere can a better refutation of this dogma be found than in the extremely important petroleum industry. The tremendous wastes of petroleum and natural gas which have occurred in that industry in years gone by, the "boom and bust" life that it has lived, due to the finding of vast new underground pools, led to the introduction in Congress in 1934, with administration backing, of the Thomas-Disney Bill. This would, if constitutional, have given power to the Federal government to regulate the daily production of petroleum from every oil well in America. It would thus take from the owners, and from the states in which petroleum is a vital part of their economy, the control of this resource. It was said that irremediable ruin faced the industry for lack of the United States washing the dirty petroleum laundry of the States.

I served on the Committee of the Congress that considered that question. Instead of recommending Federal action, our committee encouraged an interstate compact between the principal petroleum states under which they might work out these questions. The compact was formed, Congress gave its consent to it, and common action under the common pact has, up to this writing at least, worked out very satisfactorily. All without turning over the entire matter to Washington bureaucrats.

The interstate compact is one of several answers to those who say that "our antiquated constitution leaves us helpless to deal with problems of great national concern" and that the power to deal with matters that transcend state boundaries *must exist somewhere*. It does.

The compact is a device authorized by the men who drafted the Federal Constitution in 1787 for accomplishing matters over which no state separately has effective power to end. The interstate compact is in effect a treaty between states in their sovereign capacities. It helps to span the twilight zone between state and Federal authority. It demonstrates that the men who wrote the Constitution of the United States way back in the "horse and buggy days" were not so shortsighted as some of their modern critics pretend.

In April 1938 the Supreme Court of the United States handed down an extremely important decision, upholding the binding effect of an interstate compact entered into between Colorado and New Mexico in 1923, with respect to the use of the water of the La Plata River. With this decision, many problems with respect to interstate streams can be adequately settled by common action of the states lying in the watershed of the river—all without rushing to Washington.

Boulder Dam, dealing with the waters of the Colorado River, one of the greatest engineering feats in history, is the result of an interstate compact among seven states. The Port of New York Authority, so familiar to all who watch the vast water-borne traffic of our greatest seaport, is the result of a compact between the states of New York and New Jersey and not an act of Congress.

All 48 states have authorized or entered into compacts or treaties among themselves with respect to different matters, including such subjects as the growing and marketing of tobacco, hour and wage legislation, child labor, etc. The virtue of a compact or uniform state legislation, or reciprocal state legislation where one state grants certain benefits to the citizen of another state if that other state grants reciprocal benefits to the citizens of the first, is that no state becomes irrevocably handcuffed to Federal control. The destiny of its industries and its citizens is not put at the hazard of votes cast in a distant legislature by men who have no immediate interest in the problems of the state particularly involved and in which the state has only a few votes. It is one thing, for example, for Indiana and Michigan to take common action with respect to problems common to these two states by which the complete control of these problems is left to their own state legislatures or other public bodies, rather than in the Congress of the United States where out of 531 votes in both the House and the Senate, the State of Indiana, for example, has only 14 votes.

States hesitate to throw the key down the well by surrendering all of their power to Washington which, once done, could not be recovered except by a majority vote in both Houses of Congress, plus executive approval, or, in case of a constitutional amendment, without consent to ratify concurred in by 35 other states. Acting by themselves, however, either individually or cooperatively they may still go far in solving these "modern problems" and yet retain the key to their own destiny in their own hands.

But we have not yet exhausted the alternatives to Federal empire. In 1803 when Thomas Jefferson was President of the United States, interested as he was in the eventual extinction of human slavery, Congress passed a law "prohibiting the importation of any negro . . . into any state where by the laws thereof their admission is prohibited." Jefferson signed the Act. It became the law of the land. By passing it Congress did not itself attempt to say whether negro slaves might or might not be imported from one state into the other. It left that decision to the people of the particular state. But, by passing this act it made effective the state prohibition of the importation of slaves. It took out from the protection of the interstate commerce clause of the Federal Constitution the transportation of slaves which at that time were property the same as any other chattels. This historic precedent of Jefferson's time is of high value today. It not only demonstrates that our fathers were not as dumb as some of the brain trusters make out, but it points the solution to many similar problems today with reference to which a state, acting through its own state legislature, might desire to take action to protect its own interests.

This alternative to empire has been immensely strengthened by two recent decisions of the Supreme Court of the United States upholding acts of Congress known as the Hawes-Cooper Act, and the Ashurst-Sumners Act. These acts were passed by Congress along the line of the Jeffersonian precedent of 1803.

For example, goods made by prison labor. The competition of prison made goods with goods made by free labor has become so important that some 30 states representing 90 millions of the population of the United States have dealt with it. But,—if Ohio by act of its state legislature forbade the sale in Ohio of brooms, shoes, etc. made by convicts in Ohio prisons, in order to protect the brooms and shoes made in Ohio by free labor, Ohio was still confronted with prison labor goods made in other states of the union being shipped into Ohio in interstate commerce and thus nullifying the beneficial effects intended by its own legislation.

Problems such as these led to the passage of the acts of Congress referred to. The effect of these acts was to take away the protection of the interstate commerce clause of the Federal Constitution, as to which the Federal government has exclusive authority, from prison labor goods made in other states being shipped into Ohio in violation of her own law. It will be seen that Congress did not undertake, itself, to say whether prison labor made goods should or should not move and be sold in interstate commerce in each and all of the 48 states of the Union. Congress said only that if a state forbade such sale in its own jurisdiction that goods could not come in from the outside and render ineffective the state legislation. This gives effectiveness to state legislation but at the same time leaves the determination of the question whether prison labor made goods should be sold in a particular state entirely to the people of that state. By changing, amending, or repealing its own act, the state can retain control of its own affairs.

These acts of Congress were held constitutional by the Supreme Court of the United States by unanimous vote by two decisions in March 1936 and January 1937.

The very great importance of these decisions is apparent. They appear to be "enabling acts" for states in the field of social legislation to protect workers, to build up labor standards and deal with other modern problems. For it would seem that if it is constitutional for Congress to pass an act to enable a state to exclude goods made by prison labor from competing with goods made by the free labor of the state, it would be equally constitutional to pass legislation enabling a state to forbid competition with the free labor of that state of goods made by child labor, or by adult sweatshop labor, etc. working under labor standards in other states inferior to those of the particular state.

This was the way many thought Congress should have proceeded in the last session with respect to wage and hour legislation. The benefit of proceeding by this course seems obvious.

If, for example, in its textile factories, Massachusetts forbade the employment of labor more than 40 hours a week, or at a wage less than some prescribed minimum, the legality of which state legislation seems now conceded, Massachusetts could protect its own market, its own labor, its own industries, against like goods made by substandard labor coming in from some other state. This would protect the market of the high labor state. At the same time it would permit freedom with respect to its own affairs to states whose geographical or industrial situation is peculiar. It would not immediately force every state in the union into a Federal straitjacket but it would protect the high labor standard state from competition from other low labor standard states. But in so doing it would be a powerful inducement to the substandard labor states gradually, and as they could without violent economic dislocations, to improve their own labor standards for the purpose of qualifying their products to enter the markets in the states of the higher labor standards.

If we had proceeded along this course, it seems probable that within a few years all states, the prosperity of whose industries depend upon selling goods in other states, would enact legislation themselves to improve their labor standards. If the recently passed Federal wage and hour legislation is held unconstitutional by the United States Supreme Court, as to which there are important precedents for so holding, it would seem to be the part of wisdom to then go back to the Jeffersonian precedent of 1803.

The same general principle was applied some 25 years ago with respect to the shipment of intoxicating liquor into a state which had forbidden such sale by act of its own legislature. Congress took action to remove from the protection of the interstate commerce clause intoxicating liquor to be shipped into a state which forbade its sale.

The work being done by the American Arbitration Association should not be overlooked in the important field of labor disputes which, not settled, often lead to strikes and layoffs affecting the economy of many states with repercussions throughout the entire nation. This Association tries to keep labor and other disputes from reaching open hostilities or from going into court where the parties often feel obliged to take inflexible positions to "keep face." This Association is establishing itself in the public confidence as an instrument for the adjustment of the delicate fabric of confidence between management and labor, in which government officials, due to political pressure of all sorts, are a poor substitute, as we are now learning.

The Association offers a panel of arbitrators chosen solely for integrity, impartiality, and competence, who serve without compensation. It offers its facilities on precisely equal terms, on equally fair conditions, to both management and labor. In view of the great dissatisfaction of important groups of our people in the procedure and decisions of the National Labor Relations Board, in which the Federal government tried to act, the effort to promote voluntary industrial arbitration before arbitrators of the highest integrity and in whose decisions all interested parties have confidence, holds momentous promise.

I am glad to say that officials of both the American Federation of Labor and the Committee for Industrial Organization are speaking well of the work being done by the American Arbitration Association.

In commenting upon the work of this body, Mr. Raymond Moley recently said:

"What the American mind needs most is a restoration of its old habit of dependence upon voluntary, unofficial methods of social and economic betterment. The hopes and fears of all of us have too long been centered in what the government is doing to or about us. Without realizing it, a large proportion of the people of this country have become, not the vassals of an omnipotent state, as frightened pessimists say, but something almost as bad—the intellectual vassals of the idea of an omnipotent and omniscient stateism. And that is not good for individuals or for the state.

"One simple remedy for this malady that comes to mind immediately is the nurturing of the old virtue of self-reliance—a self-reliance that finds expression in voluntary, self-sustaining associations."

As another "alternative to Federal empire," hundreds of millions, if not billions of dollars of business between producers and consumers in the different states are now covered by trade practice agreements voluntarily worked out by representative bodies of various industries to prevent unfair trade practices. Few of our people seem to realize that these trade practice agreements ante-dated N.R.A. and did not come to an end with the decision of the Supreme Court holding N.R.A. unconstitutional. These trade practice agreements to eliminate unfair trade practices by voluntary agreement of the representatives of an industry began many years ago and still continue. Eleven years ago the Division of Unfair Trade Practices of the Federal Trade Commission was set up for the purpose of assisting industries in working out trade practice agreements which are in the public interest. Under the assistance of the Federal Trade Commission some 200 industries have now undertaken the establishment of Fair Trade Practice Rules and Agreements. This is another illustration of the old adage that "where there is a will there is a way"—a voluntary way rather than a compulsory way.

Enough has been said along this line. We can go down the Hamiltonian trail as important persons in Washington, D. C., are now doing and wind up with rigid and inflexible controls over all the diverse industries of this vast country. Careful students of the present trend believe this course will lead almost certainly to the totalitarian state in America which cannot be run except by some form of dictatorship. Or, we can reverse our course and go back to the old safe Jeffersonian road.

We can have either an ironclad empire or an inseparable union of indissoluble states "diverse as the billows and one as the sea." Such is the choice. We cannot have both.

The problem is not whether workable alternatives to empire can be found. They exist. The real problem is whether our people have the courage and the intelligence to use them.

CHAPTER 20

THE PRICE OF A PLANNED ECONOMY

We have been unwilling to face the final fact. We fool ourselves with the naive belief that we can have the benefits (?) of collectivism and by some hocus-pocus have our freedom also. But the final fact is that collectivism and liberty cannot live in the same land.

This I think can be demonstrated as certainly as a problem in Euclid. If we can prove it, the next question before America is whether we are willing to pay the price—the loss of liberty. A collateral question is whether we gain permanent values in our standards of living. Study of the problem will show I think, that by substituting collectivism for free enterprise, we have not only substracted from our liberty, but *added* to our insecurity.

If we are to give up our liberty let us do so with cold calculations. We owe that much to our children if not to ourselves. For we give up their liberty also. For ourselves we may be willing to gamble our fortunes on a Pied Piper's tune, but we hold the future of our boys and girls *in trust*.

At this point, I wish the reader had at his elbow Walter Lippmann's "The Good Society." Mr. Lippmann demonstrates convincingly that a planned economy cannot succeed without martial law or its equivalent. That is the price. We have not had nerve enough to pay that price, or even to face the fact that that price must be paid. One reason the planned economy of the last five years is now in a state of near collapse and requires constant financial blood transfusions is that we have blanched at the final barrier, the regimentation of labor, the compulsion to work at a wage level fixed by the state.

There is nothing new in this. Old Sam Gompers was wise enough to see the end result, was honest enough to proclaim it, and brave enough to have nothing to do with it.

Under martial rule, to summarize Mr. Lippmann, the planning board might conceivably estimate the amount of cloth necessary to clothe the people; the planners could count the plannees, measure the six-footers, the five-footers, the lean, the fat, etc., and calculate roughly the requisite yardage of cloth. If the cloth were brown khaki and nothing else, the scheme might work. It is done in fact in clothing an army and some of the uniforms actually fit!

But if the khaki were both brown and blue and the plannees *had their choice of colors,* no board on earth could estimate with accuracy the amount of brown khaki and the amount of blue khaki that would be demanded.

Upon this simple freedom of choice the whole gigantic superstructure of a planned economy founders as a ship upon a reef. The French Revolution came to an end, it is said, when the women got tired of wearing blue! Our statesmen may think they can regiment the men but I want to be around when they tackle our women!

In this simple illustration of brown and blue khaki, you may say that the planner can depend on last year's proportion of choice between brown and blue *pretty closely.* But to the extent that it is not exact you immediately have the same "wastes of capitalism" you have now,—a surplus of brown khaki going to the bargain basement and rush orders going to the factory for more blue.

So you have not eliminated the wastes of free enterprise. And what virtue is there in an official badge to make the planner more competent to estimate future demand for brown and demand for blue, than the man who tries to plan production for private enterprise?

And you have just begun. Other cloth than khaki will be bought if consumers are free to choose, and other colors than brown or blue. And prices will vary. Price makes choice as well as color. As price affects choice it affects volume also. Low price means large volume; high price means small volume if the consumer is free to spend his pennies to what he thinks is his best advantage.

How about women's shoes and hats! What a headache they would give the official planner! And then to go from khaki, shoes, hats, to plan the choice of a free consumer for all of the hundred thousands of articles available for purchase in our stores. Think, for example, of a Montgomery Ward or Sears Roebuck catalogue with the thousands of articles there advertised, each with different grades and prices, a total in one catalogue alone of literally thousands of choices to a single buyer. Who is to allocate the production of all of these items? Who is going to determine in advance whether the person reading the catalogue will decide to buy a hat rather than a dress, or skates for Junior rather than paint for the chicken coop?

So we come to the final fact. When you regulate production you must regulate consumption. And when you regiment consumption you must *control the consumer*. You must take from him his freedom of choice. You have no choice except to take from him his freedom of choice. You, Mr. Official Planner, cannot tolerate a "consumers' strike." The word "regimentation" may, from much repetition, wear its corners smooth, but the fact of regimentation means *the regiment*.

We are learning this in the slow and costly school of experience where fools get their diplomas. We started a "controlled abundance" in wheat and cotton only. We attempted to increase the price of wheat by decreasing the supply of wheat. We attempted to force the consumer to bid more for wheat, if he ate wheat. But as price goes up, at a certain point the consumer will refuse to buy. Having still his constitutional freedom of choice, he will buy wheat substitutes instead, rye, barley, rice, buckwheat, etc. This throws the wheat plan out of kilter. So the planners are forced to control the production of substitutes for wheat, and the substitutes for the substitutes. And in order to control the substitutes the planner will also have to control the producers of the substitutes. Time will tell what success, if any, will greet his effort.

The same with cotton. Stop planting of cotton and the planter grows peanuts. This throws the peanut business out of kilter, so peanuts must be controlled. The farmer then switches from peanuts to potatoes. This causes a surplus of potatoes, the potato market collapses and a new act is rushed through Congress to fine and imprison anyone who grows or buys bootleg potatoes. Planned economy has a noble sound but it leads to the guard house. Under it, conformity is the only patriotism. Its only congenial climate is the war spirit.

Let me repeat. In equipping an army the only problem is what goods are needed and how much. There is no problem of what can be sold. The consumer, the soldier, is rationed. If he refuses the rations he starves in the guard house or is shot.

The free market place disappears as planned economy gains ground and it cannot gain ground if there remains the market place where a prospective buyer may choose what to buy, or whether to buy or save.

How can the general staff of a planned society—in a land where liberty exists—determine how many houses, and what kind of houses, and how many of each kind shall be built, and at what price each shall be sold? The citizen and his wife may not like the kind of house or the price. They may decide to continue renting for another year or buy an automobile instead. And if they decide to buy an automobile who will tell them what kind of an automobile?

Deep as we already are in attempting a planned economy in agriculture the next thing we hear of, and it will inevitably follow, will be allocation of production in industry. It will astonish many to learn that by a statute of Congress, passed in 1937, we have for the first time in the nation's history, already attempted to allocate production in industry. I refer to the Act relating to the refining of sugar.

But the refining of sugar, the determination by bureaucracy which refiners shall refine how much sugar, is just the beginning. Let us inquire how allocation of production in industry generally will work. In my home town the Studebaker car is made. Who determines how many Studebakers are sold in any one year? How many Buicks, Fords, Plymouths, Chryslers, or Nashes? The final decision is made by the consumer and, let me repeat, his wife.

The struggle for the consumers' dollar between competing units in an industry, by offering most and best for least, determines the allocation of total automobile production under a free competitive system. It is a competition of excellence and service as well as price. Under its stress excellence goes up and price comes down. New inventions are encouraged and new inventors. Because quality goes up, quantity goes up. No one has a monopoly. No one holds the umbrella of paternalism over industrial senility. In this process the inefficient producer goes to the wall, as dozens of automobile companies have gone to the wall. The efficient producer survives *and efficiency survives*. It may be tough on the buggy business, but mankind moves the faster.

As against this struggle for the consumers' dollar by offering most and best for least which is the keynote of the free enterprise system, political planning of industrial production is the proposed alternative. It is the only alternative. That is so whether industry is privately owned and politically managed, or publicly owned and managed.

Some government bureau, that is some man, some human being, some person liable to err, some person liable to be influenced, will estimate the anticipated total demand for next year's automobiles. He will say to Studebaker,—"Of that total you may produce 100,000; to Ford, 300,000, etc. When you shall have produced your quota, Mr. Studebaker, *lay off your men.* We will not tolerate excessive inventories. We will not tolerate over-production of your automobiles because if we do, it will disrupt our plans to produce oil burners, or refrigerators, or cooling systems."

When this government official has told Studebaker how many cars he may produce for next year's market, and when that number of cars has been produced, Studebaker then stops production. *There is then a lockout of Studebaker workers, a lockout by government!*

If Studebaker workers are then idle, will they be any happier knowing that their idleness has been caused by some decree in Washington, than if it were caused by the hazards of free enterprise? It is one thing for government to fix maximum hours and minimum wages, but when Studebaker has reached its allocation, government then closes the factory and that determines not maximum hours but *no hours at all and no wage at all* until another year's production rolls around. How will the worker like that?

He will not like it. And if he says so *with votes,* what then? Will he be permitted to say so—*with votes?* Ask the German worker.

Assuming that the automobile industry still remains in private ownership, the competitive struggle for the automobile market will still go on but it will be transferred from the free market place where consumers decide whether to buy Studebakers or Buicks, or no car at all. It will be transferred to some bureau office in Washington. The struggle there will be to convince the bureaucrat that Studebaker's allocation should be increased and Buick's allocation decreased, or vice versa. Each automobile unit will struggle for a larger share of the national market before the bureau chief, the same as they struggle for their larger share before the consumer in the free market place.

What happens when this transfer of the struggle takes place? The company with the biggest "drag" at Washington, with the biggest lobby, with the most highly paid lawyers; the company that has the "ear" of the national party chairman, or makes the largest contribution to the campaign fund, or buys the most national convention books, will get the bigger allocation. The company with less influence in Washington, or no influence at all, will have its allocation cut. And when that company's allocation is cut the *amount of work available to its workers is cut,* and the amount of wages distributed to the merchants in the town in which they live is cut. As an inevitable consequence, the whole standard of living, the whole question of good times or bad times in the city in which that company is located, and where its employees live will be affected adversely by the decision made at Washington.

The company with the big pull at Washington that gets the big allocation in the automobile market, then has nothing more to fear. It has, to the extent of its allocation, *a monopoly on the market—a monopoly created by government!*

Having a monopoly on the market, the former necessity of pleasing the prospective customer by offering a better and better car, at a lower and lower price, is gone. The competition of excellence ends. The advancing standard of living through offering a better car at a lower price comes to an end also. Furthermore, what happens to the new invention and the new inventor who would like to break into the field then occupied by the industrial giants who have their pull at Washington? The new invention, the new idea, is frozen out—and the inventor. His place in the sun is gone. His chance to compete, to survive, is gone.

Consequently when we argue against this whole philosophy of a planned economy, we are not arguing for the industrial giant, for "big business." They will have ways and means to *look after themselves as they always have throughout history.* In olden time the court favorite never lacked his place in the sun. The man who had "friends at court" did not suffer. But the little man did suffer. He did not have "friends at court." The man with the new idea could not get the ear of the king. He could not break through the circle of favorites, courtiers, and courtesans. Consequently the standard of living did not rise because society was denied the benefit of the thousands of new ideas which are released by free enterprise.

It seems plain that this whole philosophy of a planned economy is taking America straight back to the old system of the king and his court and his favorites, and the graft and corruption of the purchased privileges of centuries ago.

But our difficulties have only just begun. We have not only the improbability if not the impossibility of a pure and disinterested bureaucratic decision in this matter of allocation; we have not only this matter of freedom of choice of the consumer. We have also the question of freedom of the worker to work or not work at a *wage satisfactory to him*. Unless the advocates of a planned economy are willing to pursue their theory with inexorable logic to its inevitable end, that is, *the control of the worker* and the wage that determines his standard of living, they must fail.

Let me illustrate. If, after allocating 100,000 new automobiles to the "X" car and 200,000 to the "Y" car, suppose the workers at the "X" factory strike for an increase of wages. What then? No "X" cars would then be produced. What happens? The consumer who had been planning to buy an "X" car, and not being able to get it will decide to buy a "Y" car. This throws out of kilter the allocation previously made of "Y" cars and calls for more workers to produce more of these cars. How are you going to stop it? You cannot stop it, unless government forbids the worker at the "X" factory from striking, or the worker at the "Y" factory from making more cars. There is no way to maintain the allocation of production between "X" and "Y" in place unless that factor is controlled also. You are working against water seeking its level. If all automobile workers in all plants struck as they have a right to do under a free enterprise system, then the public, not being able to buy cars will decide to buy refrigerators, or electric washers, or something else, and this in turn throws out of kilter the whole planned economy and allocation of production in refrigerators, washers, etc.

These are merely a few of the difficulties involved in the "production for use" doctrine so much talked about today. Its advocates have not thought the problem through. For every difficulty in a free enterprise system which they think they are correcting, they are creating new and unsolvable difficulties under a planned economy system, that is, unless worker and consumer *are controlled and liberty is gone*. "Production for use" is actually the new label for Communism.

There is no way to make planned economy work with much success in a land where liberty exists. Suppose that after the 100,000 "X" cars are produced and are in the warehouse, the public refused to buy. They prefer the "Y" car with its new streamlining, or its new electric earmuffs, and buy "Y" cars and leave the "X" cars in the warehouses. How will the advocates of "production for use" get rid of the cars in the warehouse? When you think the thing through, planned economy does not eliminate a single difficulty of the free enterprise system. In addition, it creates new difficulties, chief of which is trying to guess how much of the national market the government bureaucrat will allocate to "X" and how much to "Y." This creates a new unpredictable for factory management to try to anticipate when they place their orders months ahead for raw material, steel, glass, rubber, cotton, etc. After the allocation is made suppose the workers strike and obtain an increase in wages. Unless the wage increase is neutralized by an increase in efficiency, it must in time be reflected in the cost of the car and as cost goes up sales go down. This again throws the allocation out of kilter. All planned economy reasoning is based upon the implied assumption not only of a controlled production which means the control of labor, but a controlled market, and in addition, is based upon the philosophy of scarcity and defeat.

In a period of scarcity, you can ration the things absolutely indispensable to maintain life, as you would ration a besieged garrison in time of war or a countryside in time of famine. You can hand out to each person, each day, so much black bread, so much bacon, so much salt. If the only clothing you have is khaki you can make everybody take it and "like it." They "like it" however, because of necessity only. They do not like it as a matter of free choice.

But, as Mr. Lippmann points out, the fundamental characteristic of a rising standard of living is that as it rises a constantly increasing fraction of the family income goes to buy non-essentials; pictures, rugs, sporting goods, pleasure cars, electric refrigerators, etc., etc. You might allocate the use of beans and bread when beans and bread are all there is; you might plan a barrack room living for a civilian population in time of scarcity by rationing out the daily quota of supplies, but *no one wants to live in a barrack room civilization!* We want a constantly rising standard of living, the purchase and use of more and more of the *non-essentials* which add comfort and pleasure to human happiness. If, therefore, our people are still to be free to dispose of their surplus incomes voluntarily, deciding on a rug in place of a picture, or a flower garden in place of a garden seat, who then is wise enough to plan, or even guess, what thirty million families will do with seventy, eighty, ninety, one hundred billion dollars worth of income.

You can plan your economy (if at all) only when you control the consumer as you would uniform a soldier and control the worker as you would give orders to a soldier. This, however, is the end of freedom for labor. It is the end of labor unions. It is the end of collective bargaining. It is the end of every means and mechanism by which labor throughout the years has increased its standard of living. Under the planned economy the worker becomes the peon of the state.

But as long as the worker is free to work, or not to work, and at a wage which the worker decides upon rather than the planner, you cannot have "production for use"; you cannot have control from any capital. It is only conceited sophomores in government offices who even dream that it is possible. A planned economy *to meet a free demand* makes just as much sense and no more than the mumbling of an idiot.

You can talk about "the balanced load principle" under capacity operation. You can talk about "outworn political boundaries," and the "gadgets" of the checks and balances of constitutional government. You can talk about a "normal standard of consumption." And in some ivory tower, provided by a generous government at the expense of the taxpayer, far removed from the "madding crowd's ignoble strife," you can plan each and all of these things. But you cannot make them work so long as human beings are free to dispose of their work hours and their wages for considerations satisfactory to them. Meantime you have not eliminated any of the wastes of capitalism, nor cured a single difficulty in the free enterprise system. On the contrary you have destroyed the competition of excellence and price, and in so doing you have reduced the standard of living. You have put civilization in reverse gear.

One final question is, who is to do the planning? Are "the people" going to do the planning? Will they hold a town meeting and decide how many "X" automobiles will be allowed to be produced for next year's market? No, that is impossible. The planning, the allocation of "production for use," will be determined, if at all, only by a small group of men who in other times were called tyrants *because their will is the law*. Perhaps today we might have a very wise tyrant, and a very benevolent despot, with knowledge and foresight and ability to plan not possessed by the wisest managers that private industry has yet found. Perhaps! But this benevolent superman, if found, will not live forever. He may not be in office a year from now. He may not successfully plan against his own demise. What then? Will his successor be equally wise, equally just, equally incorruptible?

No, this whole philosophy of a planned economy takes us

straight back to the same old tyrannies that our ancestors once crossed the stormy North Atlantic to escape. And yet it is being sold to the American people today as a "liberal" or "progressive" doctrine, applying "new remedies to modern needs." The men who advocate it are the modern Tories.

CHAPTER 21

THE NEW SERFDOM

"If I were in a minority of one in this convention I would want to cast my vote so that the men of labor shall not willingly enslave themselves to governmental authority in their industrial effort for freedom. . . . Let the future tell the story of who is right or who is wrong, who has stood for freedom and who has been willing to submit his fate industrially to the government."

—Samuel Gompers.

"Labor must suffer as much from the control over its relationship to industry that exists in a Fascist State, like Italy or Germany, or by autocratic dictatorship as in Russia, as does private industry. Labor and Capital have a common cause to protect against autocratic usurpation of power over their destiny by governmental agency."

—William Green.

The above quotations from the men who have led the American Federation of Labor now for more than fifty years show their concern with any doctrine that leads toward collectivism.

Shortly before he died, when he had come "to close grips with eternal things" Mr. Gompers said in his last message to American Labor, "As one who with clean hands and singleness of purpose has tried to serve the labor movement honorably and in a spirit of consecration to the cause of humanity, I want to urge devotion to the principles of voluntarism. No lasting gain has ever come from compulsion."

The historic position of American labor in working out their problems has been the principle of cooperation. It has struggled for the right to sit down at the table with the managers of enterprise and discuss and agree upon matters of mutual concern to capital and labor. This is the principle of a free contract negotiated by free men, equal partners in production, prosperity and peace. One of the greatest errors made by industrial management has been that it has not freely conceded the right of collective bargaining by responsible representatives of labor who recognize the right of private property and insist upon the sanctity of a contract once agreed upon. There are few things more encouraging than the increasing willingness of management to recognize these fundamental human values. Some of these values now beginning to be widely accepted in America for the first time, have been matters of course in England for a generation.

But we are concerned here not with the democratic process of discussion and agreement but coercion and compulsion in labor relationships. Powerful groups have risen in America with such a program. Their rise has been due in part to the stubbornness of industrial leaders in refusing to concede labor's rights. Their program is to have government dictate what must be done. The only logic in this, of course, is the hope that labor will *control the government* that does the dictating. Before further going down this road in America, let us see how it has worked abroad and the possibilities of similar results in the United States.

Today powerful voices are arguing that government shall determine how much of any commodity shall be produced. This can only mean that government will eventually fix prices by statute or bureaucratic decree. It is obvious that you cannot determine how much of a commodity shall be produced unless you also determine price, because as price rises or falls the amount of the commodity taken by the consumer will inversely fall or rise. When government therefore undertakes to determine what "consumer demand" shall be for a commodity, it must also determine how much the consumer shall pay for the commodity. When we fix prices by law where do we stop? In fact once having begun why should we stop? If we do are we not bound to work injustice somewhere along the line? If we do not stop but fix prices all along the line until the line has become a full circle, who has gained? And if we do not complete the circle how many have lost?

It is at this point that the interests of labor become involved. It is here that the danger exists which Mr. Gompers had in mind. When the price of a commodity is stabilized by law, government in time, and in justice, is obliged to stabilize all of the fractions that make up the total price. How much to the landlord; how much by way of interest and dividends to invested capital; how much to research; how much to depletion, depreciation, and amortization, how much to labor in wages? Will not all these elements clamor at Washington to increase their fractions of the total at the expense of the other fractions? They will. They are doing so and will do so by political pressure, by pull, by lobbying, by favoritism, by contributions to the party war chest, by the invisible government. *Economic* questions will receive *political* answers. The larger fraction of the dollar will go to the group which at the moment has the greatest pull at Washington. This has always been so whenever government has attempted to fix prices and it will continue to be so until we breed bigger and better bureaucrats than this earth has yet spawned.

So it all depends on who at the moment controls the government. Who has the most votes? Who can employ the most highly paid and effective lobbyists? Who can reach the ear of the executive who will make the decision? Who has "friends at court"?—ominous phrase!

There is an additional danger in labor turning over these decisions to government. It is that the necessities, real or imagined, of government itself will enter into the determination of how much labor shall get or what kind of work labor shall do. If the government is committed to a huge armament program its necessities for steel, coal, petroleum, etc., and its desire to buy these commodities as cheaply as possible will enter into the determination of how much labor will get. This is not theory. We have the record of experience behind it. It is the needs of the State, the ambitions of the rulers that dictate the decisions—not the equities of the workers. "The people are converted into fuel to feed the mere machine which is the State" wrote Jose Ortega y Gasset.

Before Fascism came to power in Italy, about 1921, Italian labor through its own organizations had won collective bargaining, compulsory accident, old age, invalidity, and unemployment insurance; reduced hours of work, and secured government supported employment agencies. The condition of Italian labor was slowly but surely being improved.

Then came Fascism. All these gains won with infinite effort were wiped out; hours of work were lengthened, wages were reduced, and the standard of living of the worker was lowered. Union headquarters, newspapers, and cooperatives were destroyed. With the stabilization of the lira in 1927 began continued and drastic wage cuts. From 1927 to 1935 day wages were reduced 37%. Measured against the cost of living the purchasing power of day wages was reduced at least 15%. Actual annual earnings have declined even more. Fascist organizations were given exclusive privilege of placing workers; unemployed members of the Fascist party had the preference for the job. Funds which went into accident, old age and sickness insurance have been in one form or another taken from the beneficiary because the government had increasing use for these funds as a source of credit.

All labor disputes must go to special courts of compulsory arbitration. Resort to any other method of settling disputes as by striking is illegal. Are these labor courts free agents to dispense justice upon the merits of the case as presented by owner and worker? They are not. "In view of the political control over the courts," the judgments of the labor courts simply register secret decisions made in higher quarters. Behind the scenes—the invisible government at work. Equity, justice, fairness, decency—where are they?" "Important is not who is right, but who wins," says Dr. Goebbels, whose philosophy is "to will with cold blood the anarchy of the moral world." "A handful of force is worth a sackful of justice," says the German Ministry of *Justice!*

With respect to agricultural labor the Fascist principle is to "fix the worker to the soil." This is twentieth century feudalism, serfdom to the state. Under this policy less and less wages are paid in money and more and more in kind, i.e., in the crops grown. This changes day laborers into sharecroppers and increases share tenancy. Meantime, the concentration of land ownership in relatively few hands has become more pronounced than ever. This whole policy has resulted in crippling the bargaining strength of the worker. There has been a steady deterioration of working standards in the decade and a half since Fascism took over the reins of power. Both the quantity and quality of food available per capita has fallen appreciably. There is a reduced consumption of wheat, meat, sugar, olive oil. The eight hour day has been forgotten; real wages have been forced below their prewar level; the right to emigrate to foreign countries has been denied; the chance of becoming an independent farmer has been dimmed; and the number of workers unemployed has increased.

In Germany, the history is much the same. The government freezes prices by decree but this also freezes wages. Effective July 1st this year Field Marshal Goering has issued a decree making it "the obligation of every German National without exception to have himself assigned for a definite period by the labor offices to certain public or other works, which on account of the recent shortage in skilled and unskilled labor cannot otherwise be achieved." The German worker goes where he is ordered and does what he is told. The condition of labor in Germany today is dictated not by the equities between capital and labor but by the necessities of government itself.

It has become popular in the United States in recent years to magnify the power of public officials, as in Germany. This has led Mr. Matthew Woll, Vice-President of the American Federation of Labor to say—"History may yet say that Naziism did even more damage to the German people by the crushing of labor than by the disgraceful persecution of the Jews. Wages in Germany are now below the level at which they stood forty years ago." While unions nominally exist, they are controlled from the inside by Nazi officials. They actually assume the roles of strike breakers and policemen. The cost of living has risen by fifteen or twenty per cent since Hitler came to power in January 1933; while the average industrial wage has been reduced from 26 to 22 marks a week by deductions for taxes, insurance, etc.

How about youth? The law of June 25, 1935, states the "obligation of all German youth of both sexes to serve their people by doing useful work but not as wage earners." That is, without compensation. Hitler has, under this law, the power to mobilize annually as many young men and women between the ages of 18 and 25 as he likes and for as long a time as he likes without pay. This is "forced labor," the conscription of the worker by the state, separate and distinct from enlistment for army service. Except that the state is the master it is no different from the indentured servant which we outlawed 100 years ago. No young person in labor service is permitted to marry without the permission of the state. "The lives of all German youth belong solely to Adolf Hitler,"—so says Von Schirach, youth leader of the Reich.

How about women? If there is any group in America who ought to scrutinize with the utmost care the present drift toward collectivism and compulsion as against what Mr. Gompers called "voluntarism" it is our women. Under constitutional democracy and free enterprise American women have been raised from the status of an unpaid servant to that of a citizen entitled to an equal place with men. They are free to engage in the better-paying positions, free to enter the professions and public life. They have attained a position of equality with men greater than has ever been permitted to women under any authoritarian state since history began. Practically every disability which was formerly attached to women, single or married, as we emerged from feudalism, has been removed.

The men of blood and iron are not kind to women. They never have been. They are not now. This drift toward collectivism, if it comes in America to the same logical end that it has in other countries, will push women back to the kitchen, the barn and the field. It will turn the clock back for decades, if not for centuries.

I am indebted at this point to an article by Judith Grunfeld in "The Nation" of March 1937. Until Hitler came to power she was a member of the German trade union's research staff at Berlin. On the authority of this informed writer, Hitler made women Class B subjects. Women today are handed over defenseless to the men who hold the entire power of the state in their hands. They have been gradually pushed down from the better-paid positions into the sweated trades, thus impairing their health. Contrary to the anticipated result of helping male wage levels, the lower wages which women have been compelled to take have brought down the wage levels of men. Nevertheless the women are the ones who are discriminated against. For equal work they receive less. In bakeries their wage is 41% less; in the clothing industry 42%; chemical industry 42%; in the metal industry 41%; paper industry 43% less than a man doing the same kind of work.

Collectivism exploits women both in wages and opportunity to work. They have been practically frozen out from the professions and from public life. The work of both men and women is determined by the needs of the state. As Dr. Goebbels, Minister of Propaganda, says, "Guns are more important than butter." Freedom of expression has been denied to women not only with reference to labor relationships but to the greater questions of war and peace and the use of their babies as the future cannon fodder of the state. Such is the fate of women in Germany, many of whom fought to establish the very dictatorship under which they now suffer. A few of their more gifted members, with a courage not possessed by the men, have protested in an appeal to Hitler that "China, Japan and Turkey are far more advanced today in regard to the position of women than we are. . . . Men have led the world to an abyss and the danger still continues if one-sided rule by men is set up." They "begin to regret that in their national feeling they raised men to be unrestricted masters of the destinies of women and the nation." Such is the tragic fate of women workers in Nazi Germany. It should be an SOS across the Atlantic to the women of America.

Russia tells much the same story. The difference is that the shirts are red rather than black and there are more beards and fewer mustaches.

Such has been the fate of labor when the state is either given or seizes the power to determine the conditions of industrial relations. Mr. Gompers was right. It means not only the degradation of labor but a gradual deterioration in living standards for every one. Everybody lives in a state of fear. There is a constant blanket over initiative, invention, new ideas. If the assembly line in a Russian factory breaks down the foreman or superintendent knows that he may, however unjustly, be charged with sabotage, with the brick wall or Siberia in the background. Consequently, he initiates as little as possible. He waits for orders. He takes no chances. Production moves slowly. It has been said that more people are killed in Russia after a train wreck than in it. The result is that men do not care to rise to positions of responsibility, to become foremen, superintendents, managers, owners. And so with all of the control over labor relationships which it is possible to grant to government, the end result is that in terms of what his wage will buy of food, clothing, fuel, etc., the employed American wage earner, even in the worst years of our depression, was able to buy more of the necessities and comforts of life than the wage earner in any totalitarian state.

The promissory notes of the authoritarians are coming to protest. With more power than has been entrusted to man in the western world for generations, we have in Europe today less of stability, less of security, less of prosperity, and certainly less of freedom and civil rights, than men have known in centuries. The movement toward centralization of power is not liberal. It is reactionary.

Despite the glowing promises of these world shakers, these modern Caesars of the jutting jaw, these men of blood and iron, these madmen hearing voices in the air, what is the result of these tragic years? It can be stated in a few words. It is a will-o'-the-wisp. It is a mirage. "Follow me. Behind the concentration camps of peace and the cemeteries of war there is the Promised Land!"

CHAPTER 22

STATES' RIGHTS AND RESPONSIBILITIES

"What has destroyed liberty and the rights of man in every government which has existed under the sun? the generalizing and concentrating all cares and powers into one body, no matter whether the autocrats of Russia or France, or the aristocrats of a Venetian Senate. And I do believe that if the Almighty God has not decreed that Man shall never be free (and it is blasphemy to believe it) that the secret will be found to be in making himself the depository of powers respecting himself, so far as he is competent to them, and delegating only what is beyond his competence . . . to higher and higher orders of functionaries, so as to trust fewer and fewer powers, in proportion as the trustees become more and more oligarchial."

—Jefferson.

I have said that "free enterprise" is a misnomer. If enterprise is free it is controlled by competition. In the same way "States' Rights" is an unfortunate expression. It has done immeasurable harm to our form of government. It is an expression which obscures the real issue. You cannot interest people in abstractions. Geographical areas have no rights. It is only human beings who have rights.

What is really meant by "States' Rights" is this: "Where shall power be placed? Where will the power which necessity forces us to turn over to public officials be exercised most wisely, economically, and safely to the human beings over whom the power is exercised?"

To make a simple illustration—is traffic better regulated from the city hall or by the traffic officer at the intersection? Is it better regulated at the state capitol than at the city hall? Is it better regulated at Washington than at the state capitol? Will you be more satisfied with the education of your children when the schools they attend are managed by a board of trustees whom you have the right to put in or out of office, who live in your community and with whom you can confer with reference to your children and their teachers? Is power better exercised by officials close to the affairs they attempt to manage and who are required to give an account of their stewardship at frequent elections? Were the people better satisfied with respect to regulating the liquor traffic to have the necessary power lodged in the state governments? or in the Federal government?

The division of power between national and state governments is a very practical matter. It is not a theory. Some followers of Jefferson make the mistake of thinking that "States' Rights" is some sort of fixed pattern, a rigid concept. It is not. We live in a changing world. Jefferson lived in a changing world. Jefferson favored the "more perfect union" of the Constitution of 1787 as against the loose Articles of Confederation under which the Revolutionary War had been fought.

Our third president was a realist. He knew that it was better for certain powers to be concentrated in Washington. He was equally convinced that it was disastrous to concentrate all power in Washington. If he had been living today, it seems quite certain that he would have favored the control of the allocation of radio wave lengths at a central point. He was too practical a man to argue that it should be done by 48 state commissions. He would have recognized the danger that goes with this concentration of power over radio, a danger that would cease to be theoretical if the central government were ever seized by an American Hitler. Nevertheless it is a matter of necessity.

Not satisfied with the members of a local school board some people want to take power from them and give it to other human beings at the state capitol. Not satisfied with their decisions they would take the power from them and give it to other human beings still further off. Already many voices are clamoring for Federal control of education. They say that education has become "national." We must not leave it to the "backward states." In the chapter "Exhibit A, Washington, D. C." I have indicated how the Federal government handles education in the city of Washington.

It is the old story. "The far off cows have the longest horns; the grass on the other side of the fence is greenest."

It should be recognized, however, that every transfer of power to the Federal government is a subtraction of power from state and local officials. This means that it is a subtraction of *your power,* that is, the power to vote out of office public officials in whose administration *you* have lost confidence. Your vote is diluted as officials get further from you. Most of this trend toward centralization is an escape philosophy. It is a species of passing the buck. It is the law of the lazy. Subject to such common sense exceptions as Federal control of the radio, it raises the old question whether our people have lost the capacity, the character and the will for self-government.

Have we lost the "vigilant and manly spirit which actuates the people of America, a spirit which nourishes freedom and in turn is nourished by it," as described in the Federalist Papers? No one can answer this question except the people themselves.

When the Constitution was signed, Benjamin Franklin was asked "Is it a monarchy or a republic?" He answered, "A republic, if we can keep it." A little later General Washington, writing to La Fayette, said the new government was in no danger of degenerating into a monarchy, aristocracy or any other form of despotism "so long as there shall remain any virtue in the body of the people." On another occasion Franklin said the new government "can only end in despotism as other forms have done before it when people have become so corrupted as to need despotic government, being incapable of any other."

Some people look to the Constitution and courts to protect their liberties. It is a vain hope. It is a task they can perform only for a short time. In the end only the people can save their liberties. Courts and constitutions are, at the last, nothing but the mirror in which the spirit of the age is reflected.

But if, as Edmund Burke said, society is "a great and silent compact between the dead, the living, and the unborn," we and the people of the world could well pause in our mad rush towards the streamlined Caesars to reflect upon the legacy of self-government bequeathed to us by our fathers. Shall "the unborn" be deprived of *their* chance to preserve it? Shall we break our "compact" with our children? It is a great legacy. Our fathers were right in insisting upon keeping close to the people just as much of the power over them as is possible.

In 1926, Calvin Coolidge said, "No method of procedure has ever been devised by which liberty could be divorced from local self-government. No plan of centralization has ever been adopted which did not result in bureaucracy, tyranny, inflexibility, reaction and decline." All history, ancient and modern, supports this statement.

A distinguished chronicler of the downfall of Rome said,—

"The system of bureaucratic despotism, elaborated finally under Diocletian and Constantine, produced a tragedy in the truest sense, such as history has seldom exhibited; in which, by an inexorable fate, the claims of fanciful omnipotence ended in a humiliating paralysis of administration; in which determined effort to remedy social evils only aggravated them until they became unendurable; in which the best intentions of the central power were, generation after generation, mocked and defeated by irresistible laws of human nature and by hopeless perfidy and corruption in the servants of government."

This drift toward the centralization of power is not inevitable. Much of it comes from the sheer laziness and cowardice of state and local officials. They want money to spend but they *don't want to have to face their people with the tax bill!* So by political legerdemain the idea is developed that if the money comes from Washington it costs nothing. It is an effort to postpone payday and "pass the buck" to someone else to collect the bill.

Another influence toward centralization is the age-old disposition of distant bureaucrats to find new excuses for perpetuating themselves, to extend their jurisdiction and put more relatives on the payroll. Another influence referred to elsewhere is the effort of poor states to transfer to themselves revenues from prosperous states. None of these things have any real relation to the question itself—"Where shall power be deposited to the best advantage of those governed?"

No one who has seen the pull and haul in the national legislature by pressure groups and sectional interests, which bring into play factors which have little or nothing whatever to do with the merits of the question under consideration, can have very much faith that people are better off if the power over their own affairs is transferred from their own agents to the representatives of other constituencies and sections. A matter affecting Indiana, for example, under self-government will be decided by the legislature of the State of Indiana, every member of which is an Indiana man, responsible to Indiana citizens; or it may be decided at Washington, D. C., in another legislature of 531 members in which Indiana has 14 members only and where Indiana interests are overwhelmingly outvoted.

This clash of interests was very noticeable with reference to the last agricultural bill. Should dairy farming be transferred from the sections of the United States where it has naturally developed, to other sections of the country? How many cows should a Southern cotton farmer be allowed to have? Should the cotton farmer in California take the big cut in cotton acreage or the cotton farmer in South Carolina? These questions, when the power to determine them is centered in Washington, are decided not by the law of economics, but by the single question—who has the most votes? It was said that passage of the Potato Bill and the first Guffey Coal Bill was due in part to a "trade" between Congressmen from potato districts and Congressmen from coal districts, each voting for what the other wanted.

Similar questions rise in a dozen forms. If these questions are to be determined by "who has the most votes at Washington" the California citrus trade may be curtailed for the benefit of Florida oranges and lemons, or vice versa. The location of industries, if industry is to be allocated, and the welfare of factory workers will be subjected to similar hazards. Industry, farming, etc., will be shuffled back and forth, depending on what section has the most votes, can grant the most favors from public treasuries, or impose prohibitive conditions elsewhere, such as dictated freight rates.

The waste of public money and the temptation to waste it becomes greater the further removed the spenders are from those who pay the bill. The State of Maine, for example, would never have voted to harness the tides of Passamaquoddy, although Maine alone could have possibly obtained any benefits if that engineering nightmare had been completed. *Centralized government is always extravagant.* It is a blank letter of credit. The results are vicious in the extreme.

Transfer these powers to the central government, and petroleum, natural gas, and coal will be competing for the markets of America by votes on Capitol Hill. The attempt to plan business will depend more and more on guesswork as to what Congress or government bureaus will do. The more uncertainties along this line, the less business and the less prosperity. We are feeling this today.

But despite all these arguments that amply justify the distribution of power which our fathers made between state and nation, the tide toward centralization it not likely to be reversed unless the states and their citizens exercise the responsibilities that go with "state rights." Every right creates a responsibility. If the responsibility is not exercised the right is gone. Power flows to the hands that use it. It therefore becomes our deepest concern to improve state and local self-government in every possible way. This means, among other things, the development in the states and their local subdivisions of a strong civil or career service, protected in tenure of office, and in the integrity of their decisions. Whether government is administered at Washington or the state capitol it must deal with more and more tasks. It must regulate in the public interest more and more business. It is of profound importance to our prosperity that this regulation proceed upon the merits of the issues involved, free from political pressures.

Few things have done more to discredit state government and to operate as an excuse for centralizing power at Washington than the record of state utility commissions dealing with rails, trucks, buses, gas, electricity, telegraph, telephone, etc. State public utility commissioners should be elected or appointed for longer terms, and ways and means should be found to place them and their personnel on a strict merit basis. In only a very few states are any experience and technical qualifications required. In most states commission members are subject to removal by the political heads of the state governments who, politics being what it is, are under the temptation of being influenced by campaign contributions. Thus the spoils system sells the people down the river.

A public utility bill was before Congress in 1935. One of the arguments for it was the fact that Texas did not even *have* a public utility commission. This was a confession I did not think the Lone Star State could be happy to make. Nevertheless it illustrates that if we are to reverse this drift toward the totalitarian state in America, the 48 states and their citizens *must exercise the responsibilities that go with their rights.*

I close with two statements made to former Ambassador Richard Washburn Child, one from a Russian Communist and

the other from an Italian Fascist, both prominent men. The
Fascist said:

> "The more concentrated are the powers and the wider the
> activities of government, the better are our final opportuni-
> ties. Give us one spot where we can find the seed of power
> in the form of the army, the bureaucracy, also railroads,
> telegraphs and basic industries; that gives us our ideal
> target . . . When government has drawn into its hands
> power over production, distribution, and communication, it
> always builds a bureaucracy which taxes, irritates and med-
> dles with labor. The first result is to put into a single basket
> all that we wish to seize; the second is to irritate the over-
> taxed and impoverished mob which we will use to seize it."

The Communist said:

> "The difficulty confronting our propaganda and plans in
> America is that the political system has in it so much of
> political self-government . . . Real power in America
> politically is that of the community, the real power eco-
> nomically is that of your financial and economic system.
> That is what constitutes the obstacle to communistic ad-
> vance in America."

But so-called "liberals" (God save the mark!) are destroying
the barriers erected by our fathers against the tyranny of the
coming Caesars.

CHAPTER 23

DECENTRALIZATION OF INDUSTRY

"When we get piled upon one another in large cities, as in Europe, we shall become corrupt as in Europe, and go to eating one another as they do there. . . . The mobs of great cities add just so much to the support of pure government as sores do to the strength of the human body."

—Jefferson.

In the spring of 1937 the hosts of democracy gathered at Jefferson Island in Chesapeake Bay and some words of wisdom were uttered. The controversy over the Supreme Court Bill then raging was scarcely mentioned. But on another subject President Roosevelt expressed himself as if he were old Tom Jefferson himself. Without quoting him, it had to do with the congestion of industry and the growth of great cities.

This was strictly along the Jefferson tradition. If there was one subject that was dear to Jefferson's heart, it was the importance of men keeping close to the soil. He believed that the success of the great experiment of free government depended largely upon it. He felt that when America ceased to be predominantly agricultural and became industrial the testing time of democracy would have arrived in America. That time has come.

The Greeks were wise men. Long before the Master spoke to the humble shepherds and fisher folk around Galilee the Greeks were condensing into parables the wisdom of ages. One of their myths had to do with Antaeus, the wrestler. In Greek mythology Antaeus was never thrown by any adversary so long as he kept any part of his body, even though it were but his finger or toe, upon Mother Earth.

Only in the same way can democracy remain invincible. For want of keeping close to the soil democracy may be overthrown. Here is a great challenge to the statesmen in industry.

I walk with no one who does not hope with me that the day may come in America when slums will no longer be horrible scars upon our industrial and social frontiers, and when every laborer willing to work may have for himself and his family a home and a garden with hollyhocks along the wall, and a place for his kids to play in the sun. I would like to see a hundred county-seat towns grow up in place of one huge city. Is this possible? There is increasing evidence that science, technology and power, which heretofore have almost inevitably gravitated to great industrial centers, will in the years to come reverse gears. In other words that the trend of science and technology will be centrifugal rather than centripetal.

Heretofore the location and growth of great cities has been determined primarily by cheap transportation and access to power and raw material. Until the last century cheap transportation was by water and hence practically every great city in the world has been located on ocean, lake, river, or canal. In addition industry grew up near raw materials, such as iron deposits or around sources of power, water falls, and coal mines. Hence we have Pittsburgh and the Ruhr.

The same forces of science which heretofore have caused industry to concentrate in limited areas are now at work in the reverse direction. For example, the cost of railroad transportation from producer to consumer has been steadily reduced and its service speeded up. The internal-combustion engine gave us not only the passenger automobile but the truck, the bus, and the ribbons of concrete upon which they move. The rural free delivery, the telephone, radio, consolidated schools, and motion pictures are making available to those who live in the country the same advantages of news information, education, entertainment, good music, etc., as those who live in the city. The age of electricity, challenging the age of steam, now makes it possible to transmit power by wire over great distances, thus making it less necessary for industry to be near coal mines or waterfalls. The "grid system" permitting the exchange of electric power with the speed of light from one area to another hundreds of miles apart, is reversing the tide.

Relatively, both for industry and the family, the city no longer has the advantage over the smaller community in the country.

But over and above all this there is the urge to get back to sun and soil. These bring health and happiness. They bring peace and they bring a sense of security. They relieve the tensions of modern life. This is clearly evident by the summer migrations of the millions to the seashore, the mountains, the great state and national parks. Fathers and mothers for themselves and their children want to get away from the filth, the noise, the smoke and the tension of the great cities. Cheap and quick transportation is already doing its beneficent work.

Child idleness has now become a much more serious problem than child labor. In the city the boy has little to do. He does not even have a lawn to mow. In the country there are chores to do, and the immemorial playmates of childhood,—dogs, lambs, calves, chickens, ducks. The problem affects people in the later years of life equally, the men and women who in the cities have passed the industrial deadline. Living in smaller towns or the country, however, with a garden, our older people can be happy. Even for those who have not passed the industrial deadline the march of science and technology is shortening their working day and their working week, and again the factory worker is happier if when the whistle blows he can work his garden and grow food and flowers, berries and beauty. Because men are happier in the sunshine this movement back toward the country of which we see evidences today will tend in itself not only to prevent the problems of industry from becoming more acute, but will tend directly to solve them. It gives the worker two strings to his bow. With a one or five acre tract he can keep busy even during slack times in the factory. As Arthur Morgan, chairman of T.V.A., says in his "The Long Road," the man with his roots in the earth is like a turtle, not easily overturned; the city man is a giraffe.

Henry Ford has been blamed for many things. I shall not enter into these points of dispute. I believe, however, that as he pioneered in the cheap car, it may be recorded of him in the years to come that his pioneering in the decentralization of industry will possibly be as great a legacy as the work he has done strictly in industry itself.

It may prove to be a great good not only for industry but agriculture. The Farm Chemurgic movement is something to watch. It has infinite possibilities of transforming the farm from a producer of food alone to a source of raw materials for industry. This will provide the greatly needed new markets for the farm.

As Mr. Ford has said, "Agriculture needs a wider and steadier market. Industrial workers need more and steadier jobs. Can each be made to supply what the other needs? . . . The link between is chemistry. In the vicinity of Dearborn we are farming twenty thousand acres for every thing from sunflowers to soy beans. . . . I foresee the time when industry shall . . . draw its raw material largely from the annual produce of the fields. The dinner table of the world is not a sufficient outlet for the farmer's products. . . . I am convinced . . . that we shall grow annually many if not most of the substances needed in manufacturing. When that day comes, and it is surely on the way, the farmer will not lack a market and the worker will not lack a job. More people will live in the country. The present unnatural condition will be naturally balanced again. Our foundations will be once more laid on the land. . . . Ten years ago we started seven village industries on small water power sites. . . . The experiment has been a continuous success. Overhead cost has been less than that in the big factory, and the workers would not hear of going back to the city shops. As they are free to till land in the growing season, throughout these trying times (of the depression) they have all remained self-sustaining. Their security is produced by machine and farm, not by one alone."

Mr. P. W. Litchfield, President of the Goodyear Tire & Rubber Company said, "The trend is toward branch factories . . . in any manufacturing enterprise a point is reached where the law of diminishing returns makes itself felt. Experience has taught us that a 5000-tire plant running at full capacity with a standardized line can be just as efficient as one of 20, 30, or even 40-thousand units with a fluctuating volume."

It is too early to appraise the final result of the recent change made by the steel industry in the basing point system, "Pittsburgh plus." Many observers, however, believe that this will have a profound effect in the decentralizing of not only steel but many other allied industries.

A few decades ago practically all cement was made in the Lehigh Valley of Pennsylvania. Today every important cement company operating on a national basis has numerous plants. The meat packing industry is decentralizing. Chicago today is merely its largest center. Swift & Company, for example, operate 48 packing plants and several hundred distributing offices; Armour only a few years ago, operating with packing plants in 15 states, has recently added 12 plants in territories where it was not before represented; Union Carbide operates 160 plants; Air Reduction Company 133 plants; American Can operates 50 plants, and Continental Can nearly the same number; National Biscuit is in 32 cities; Continental Baking Company has 100 bakeries in 28 states; California Packing Corporation has 75 plants; Simmons Company (manufacturers of beds and furniture) has been decentralizing for a decade.

As industry decentralizes, of course housing decentralizes. As industry moves away from the slums, people move away from the slums.

Here is a movement undirected by government which holds great promise to government itself.

"It is not too soon" said Thomas Jefferson, "to provide by every possible means that as few as possible shall be without a little portion of land. *The small land-owners are the most precious part of the state.*"

CHAPTER 24

THE AMERICAN WAY

At present it is popular to speak scornfully of the "horse and buggy days." The century and a half, however, which followed 1776, is the greatest age in the world's history. It came from the emancipation of man—politically, industrially and economically. Since 1776 down to the World War man moved farther forward than he had since the birth of Christ. At the beginning of this age, the same tools, with few improvements, were being used in agriculture and transportation as were used in the Dark Ages or earlier.

This age abolished chattel slavery. It emancipated women; it gave them the vote; it made them citizens; it removed disabilities with respect to their property and contracts. It put an end to the indentured or "bound" servant. It created conditions where child labor was the exception and not the rule. It gave every American child free education and compelled his parents to see that he got it. A hundred years ago the standard day in factories was from dawn to dark. The same was true on the farm. By harnessing steam and electric power we now produce a greater volume of goods with less effort and drudgery than the world has ever known.

It was an age of continuing progress in the field of social legislation and in the conditions under which men and women work. It was an age which did more for the health of mankind than all previous centuries combined. It conquered the worst of the plagues. This age practically abolished illiteracy in America. It put free libraries within the reach of every citizen.

Since 1790 the standard of living, that is the amount of

goods which the dollar will buy, has increased fourfold. Since 1850 the wage of the average industrial worker has increasd from 9¢ to 59¢ per hour. Since 1870, eighteen new industries have been created giving direct and indirect employment to 10,000,000 workers. From 1884 to 1930 industrial production increased twelve times. A larger fraction of total income has gone to workers, the increase from 1850 to 1930 being from 38% to 65%. From 1890 to 1920 the wages of the industrial worker increased three times, and the purchasing power of his wages in terms of the goods they buy increased 48%. One in every seven factory workers is a shareholder in some American company.

There are 44,000,000 savings bank accounts with deposits of $24,000,000,000; 10,000,000 members of Building and Loan Associations with deposits of $8,000,000,000; counting industrial policies there are some 64,000,000 persons whose lives are insured, a total of about $108,000,000,000; more protection against the hazards of death, illness, and old age, than in all the rest of the world put together. Since 1776 America has produced three times as much wealth as existed in the entire world at that time. Today with 7% of the world's population, it has 45% of the world's wealth. In the 75 years preceding 1922, our population increased 5 times, our wealth 50 times, or 10 times as fast. Every decade during that period produced as much as the total wealth that existed in America in 1849 when gold was discovered in California.

I have never been able to understand how we accomplished all this by doing everything wrong. It raises the serious question whether it is necessary or advisable to attempt to make far-reaching changes in the political control over industry and agriculture.

We have 15,000,000 telephones, 29,000,000 radios, 11,000,000 washing machines, 9,000,000 electric refrigerators, 20,000,000 electric irons, 10,000,000 vacuum cleaners, some 26,000,000 automobiles—70% of the world's total; enough so that every man, woman and child in the United States could all ride on rubber at the same instant of time, a miracle of achievement in which bureaucrats played no part. When Hitler, Mussolini or Stalin does one-half as much, it will be twice as much as they have done!

We spend $10,000,000,000 annually for recreation. In terms of the steel worker's hours of work, a basket of food containing a pound each of bacon, beef, bread, butter, potatoes, sugar, a dozen eggs and a quart of milk can be purchased by the American steel worker in exchange for 1½ hours' work; by a similar worker in France for 3¼ hours' work; by a similar worker in England for 3¾ hours' work; by a similar worker in Sweden for 4¼ hours' work; by a similar worker in Germany for 5¾ hours' work; and by a similar worker in Italy for 10¼ hours' work. All this has been done despite serious inequities in the distribution of wealth, and despite monopolistic practices which have greatly hindered the production of wealth.

Despite these brakes upon production and competition, men, nevertheless, have struggled to sell goods. Our growth has been due to this struggle, competing for the consumer's dollar by offering most and best for least. This competition has improved the quality of goods, increased their quantity and brought down their price. In bringing down the price it has freed dollars to purchase other things.

A striking example of this is the automobile industry. Even during the depression years, from 1928 to 1936, the automobile industry produced a constantly better car, with a reduction in price to car buyers of a total sum of $637,000,000. This is equivalent to a wage increase to all buyers whether employed workers, or not, as it permitted them to use the $637,000,000 for other things. This stimulated purchases elsewhere and *employment* elsewhere. This sum so saved to consumers equals the total amount paid for all electric light and power used annually in the American home; it equals the nation's entire food bill for two weeks; the nation's entire clothing bill for one month;

the nation's entire rent bill for 2½ weeks; the nation's entire tax bill—Federal, state and local—for two weeks. It would pay three-fourths of all wages and salaries paid by the mining industry in the United States; one-third of all the wages paid by railroads; one-third of all the wages paid by other public utilities. The American free enterprise system by producing better goods at lower prices, under competitive stress, increases, directly and indirectly, the *real* wages of everyone. The same dollars buy more and better goods. This is the same as increasing wages.

This is not peculiar to the automobile industry. Last year the average American motorist paid $103 less for gasoline than in 1921. The price of his car per horse power has been reduced from $17.70 to $8.45 since 1928. Since 1912 the price of electric current has been reduced from 9¢ per k.w.h. to 4.4¢; a 50% reduction in cost and an increase in the number of customers from 4,000,000 to 27,000,000.

You can today buy a better radio for $37 than you could for $200 at the close of the World War. You can now buy two automobile tires for the amount you paid for one tire. And they are better tires.

In 1918 a 3-minute station-to-station telephone call from New York to San Francisco cost $18; today $6.50, with quicker service and far better reception. In ten years the cost of electric refrigerators has been reduced one-half, with a longer life and a smaller consumption of electricity. In 1884 aluminum cost $16 a pound and has recently been around 20¢ a pound. Railroad transportation costs less than one cent per freight ton mile, the lowest in the world for the service furnished. Truck and bus costs have been reduced 50% since the World War. A telegraph message can be sent across the continent for one-fourth of what it cost ten years ago. In 1929 you took 24 hours to fly from New York to San Francisco and paid $400 if you risked the flight; today you do it in 16 hours for $150, with a degree of safety inconceivable ten years ago.

This is the American system of free enterprise, operating

under the protection of constitutional government. It is not a perfect system. It has been ruthless in many respects. The displacement of men by machinery has often caused hardships to the individual worker, although, on the whole, machinery increases the total number of jobs. We have slums like scars in our cities; slashed over timber land; abandoned mining towns, and an inequitable distribution of wealth.

But there is no evidence that these ills cannot be cured within the American System, nor is there any evidence in America or abroad to warrant the conclusion that collectivist planning and management of our business, taking from the hands of the leaders of industry and the leaders of labor the determination of industrial policy, and transferring these decisions to politicians, will improve the lot of anybody *but the politicians*.

The presumption is all the other way. If this be true let us turn our efforts vigorously toward correcting existing evils, but do so within the system which has demonstrated for over 150 years its marvelous capacity for human improvement.

We are, in fact, the most liberal and progressive people in the world. We are conservatives only in the sense that we want to conserve our liberties and the American System which has created more wealth and brought more happiness to more people over a greater expanse of territory and for a longer period of time than the Pharaohs of Egypt, the Princes of Babylon, the Emperors of Rome, the lords of feudalism, or the streamlined Cæsars of today.

Forty centuries, said Napoleon, looked down upon his soldiers. One and a half centuries of the most successful government this world has ever seen look down upon us. That form of government is Jeffersonian. It is not collectivist. It is a democracy. It is not a dictatorship. It is free enterprise. It is not bureaucracy. It is discussion and consent. It is not tyranny. It is a government by law. It is not a government by men. It emancipates man. It does not enslave him.

It is a "republic, if we can keep it."

CHAPTER 25

INVENTORY

Two thousand years ago it was noted that certain persons found delight in standing on the shore as a ship was making its way through a dangerous strait and pointing out the mistakes of the captain. Knute Rockne noted the same phenomenon with respect to drugstore football coaches. Neither twenty centuries ago nor now has the public had much use for that kind of critic. Nevertheless when the man on the shore is a part owner of the cargo and his children are members of the crew he does have a legitimate interest in the course taken by the ship and the directions given by the captain.

For one, I am entirely willing to accept the appraisal of President Roosevelt made by the London "Economist" in October 1936. It was:

> "Roosevelt may have given the wrong answer to many of his problems but he is at least the first president in modern America who has asked the right questions."

The right questions were long overdue in 1933,—in banking, stock exchanges, sale of securities, guarantee of bank deposits, holding company racketeering, recovery of foreign trade, collective bargaining, conservation of soil fertility, housing, etc. Perfect answers have not been given to these questions but the people generally credit Congress and the President as having at least laid foundations that will suffice until time and experience point their corrections. Other matters such as labor relations and social security make only a poor approach toward objectives which the American people honestly desire, peace in industry and enough prosperity to support security.

But beyond these matters of reform, where are we? Where are we on recovery? On debt? On taxation? On the vast army of the unemployed? When will we begin to balance the budget? To live within our means? To stop borrowing from our children? When will the debts stop growing? When will the heaviest burden of peace-time taxation grow less? When will relief lines grow shorter? When will men go back to work? After the new pump priming runs out, what then? In short, when you take the borrowed money out from under, how much is left? We have recovery "on the cuff."

Something is wrong. The right answers to *these* questions have certainly not been found. And every one who has an interest in the cargo has the right to be concerned. He has the further right to offer honest criticism; constructive suggestions. The New Deal, first, second, or third, divides into two parts, reform and recovery. Most of the reform program was necessary. It has proved to be reasonably successful in correcting very many serious wrongs in the financial and business mechanisms of the nation. This part of the New Deal has been substantially Jeffersonian. In his words, it is designed to "restrain men from injuring one another." But has the recovery part of the New Deal been a success? Compared to the depth of the depression, partly; compared to the "par" period of 1923-25, no. Measured by total unemployment it has failed. Except that we have been robbing the children's bank, its failure would be even more pronounced.

The effort of the New Deal to bring about recovery has not been Jeffersonian. It has been Hamiltonian—even worse, it has embraced European philosophies which have succeeded neither in Europe nor America. It has broken Jefferson's great precept "to leave men free to regulate their own pursuits of industry and improvement." It has attempted to tell men affirmatively what they must do for their own good—not what they must *not* do to prevent other people's harm.

This is more than any government can do and do well even in

an iron dictatorship. It is impossible in a democracy. Mr. Roosevelt, when governor, pointed this out in his famous statement that there are no demi-gods at Washington with sufficient wisdom and disinterestedness of purpose to plan and operate the business of the nation.

Instead of attempting to free business, the government in the recovery side of its program has attempted to manage and control business. Where the attack should have been made was on every form of privilege that levies tribute on the freedom of the market and the lawful freedom of men. But instead of destroying privilege where it exists, we have offset it as men offset oil wells. It is easier to grant a new privilege than to withdraw the old one. To offset tariff privileges to manufacturers we have taxed factory workers to subsidize farmers. We have taxed one group of farmers for the benefit of other farmers. We tax some tenants to pay the rent of other tenants. We grant interest privileges to borrowers at the expense of investors. We tax industry to get funds to enable government to compete with it, in direct violation of the Democratic platform of 1932. We tax railroads to subsidize their competitors, waterways, highways, airways. By statute we try to hold up the price of coal at the expense of the consumers of coal. We build hydroelectric projects and thus deprive coal miners of their markets, taxing them to destroy them. We plow under fertile land and fertilize arid land. We plow under domestic cotton and subsidize foreign cotton. We reduce agricultural production to increase prices and denounce corporations for not reducing prices to increase production.

By statute or decree we fix the wage of labor and the price of goods. We adopt tax programs that favor the established and well-heeled industry at the expense of its younger and poorer competitor. We tell industry to raise prices one month, lower them the next. Under NRA we fostered monopolies and held up prices at the expense of all consumers. We support the largest governmental payroll in history at the expense of all other payrolls using social security funds for this purpose. We subsidize the unemployed at the expense of the employed.

We correct evils by multiplying them. Millions are subsidized and all are taxed to support the subsidies. It is a bootstrap recovery, a group of men bent over in a circle, each lifting with taxes the bootstraps of the man ahead.

When all the boys are given stilts will they be happy? They will not. There will be louder cries for taller stilts and the whole vicious circle of artificial prices, wages, interest, privileges, compensating privileges, counter-compensating privileges, and subsidies, will begin again.

So it goes. When cabbage is $8 a ton, Mr. Wallace buys at $9 a ton. And so with 20 other commodities. To "hold up" the price of clothing the Administration buys $10,000,000 worth.

Next year, it is said, wheat acreage will be reduced from 81,000,000 to 55,000,000 acres. How many farm hands and tenant farmers will that add to the 1939 and 1940 relief rolls?

At one time the government takes steps to prevent "distress" gasoline from "breaking" the market. This is "humanitarian." It produces the abundant life for gasoline distributors. A little later private industry is charged with "holding up" the price of gasoline. The men are arrested, tried, sentenced. They are bad citizens. "It is a mad world, my masters."

We "take care" of this group because we "took care" of that group. If one pressure group wins a concession we give equalizing concessions to other groups,—special privileges for all.

Take Mr. Roosevelt's statement, March 2, 1930—

"Now to bring about government by oligarchy . . . the sovereignty of our states must be destroyed. . . . We are safe from the danger of any such departure from the principles on which this government was founded just so long as home rule in the states is scrupulously preserved and fought for whenever it seems in danger."

In place of this sound doctrine, we have been eroding the states, their sovereignties, their responsibilities, their citizens.

We are moving government farther and farther from the citizen. This leaves him with a greater sense of confusion and impotence, and a diminishing sense of responsibility. It makes him more grasping for distant handouts, more reckless over the waste of public money. In so doing we are corroding his character,—easy money, soft people. We have undertaken to destroy the independence of the courts and have thus lessened the faith of the citizen in the integrity of the bench. We are undermining the independence of Congress and Congressmen and so bringing parliamentary government more and more into disrepute.

We have introduced the alien doctrine of the purge, that voters are not to be permitted to make a free choice of their own representatives. We teach the voter that he can have an abundant life if he votes for it. We teach the doctrine that it is the business of the government to support its citizens rather than citizens to support their government. The road to political success is to promise bigger and better pensions, subsidies, privileges, handouts.

Instead of simplifying government we have made it so complicated that no one can understand it, not even the government. The managers of our enterprise not only do not understand the tens of thousands of laws, rules, and regulations so far issued, but they cannot predict the laws and regulations which may be issued. This substitutes a government by men in place of a government by law. This makes government unpredictable. Business managers and investors are asked to become prophets, to outguess their government. In short, in the interest of recovery we have been substituting Federal Socialism, or Fascism, for free enterprise. We have been changing a Union of States into a bureaucratic empire. Inventory time is here. Has it worked?

There has been a species of recovery in consumers' goods. There has been little recovery in durable goods. Why? Because we have had only a short-range confidence. We have had confidence enough to buy for this week or month, a thirty-day confidence. But in durable goods we have nowhere near reached the level of 1923, 1924, and 1925. Why? Because we have not had a long-range confidence, a 5 or 10-year confidence. So we have the biggest bank deposits, and at the same time the fewest new houses in history. Idle money, idle men.

1923-25 is taken by the government itself as "par," 100. We have been "shooting for par." But have we approached the prosperity we had 13 to 15 years ago, a period 4 to 6 years before the great boom of '28 and '29? *We have not.* In freight car loadings, residential, business and industrial construction, locomotives, production of lumber, production of coal, new machinery, utility construction, foreign trade, imports or exports, we have at no time since 1933 approached the par of 1923-25. In some instances we have scarcely gone above 50% of the total business done at that time. Even with government subsidies, farm income has at no time equalled any one of these three years. Even with the increase of the public debt, total national income at no time has equalled what it was in one of these three years. And for the first time in our history we have gone into a second depression before we equalled the previous peak.

Since that par period of 1923-25 the population of the country has grown. We have 16,000,000 more people. We have now 114 people for every 100 we had then. If, for example, we were building 100 houses then, we should be building 114 houses now. In other words "par" ought to be 114. Instead we have not reached anywhere near 100 houses.

But what is the final test of recovery? It is the total national income, giving effect to both the increase of population and making adjustments for the fluctuating purchasing power of the dollar. The best year since 1933, of course, was 1937. It produced a gross national income of about 68.5 billions in current dollars, or about 76.3 billions in dollars of the same purchasing power as in 1929. This contrasts (using dollars of

the same purchasing power—1929) with the year 1923—
$77,411,000,000; 1924—$78,272,000,000; 1925—$81,827,000,-
000. *Even if the population had remained stationary,* 1937 did
not equal in total national income any one of these par period
years. 129,000,000 people have not had what 113,000,000 people
had then. If income measures recovery, we have not only fallen
far short of the previous peak; we have not even reached the
previous plateau.

Assuming that a population 14% greater should also have an
income at least 14% greater than we had in 1923-25, then upon
the average total national income of that par period ($79,200,-
000,000—in 1929 dollars) we should now have a national income
of $90,288,000,000. Instead, in 1937, we had, as stated, an
income of $68,500,000,000 in current dollars, or $76,300,000,000
in 1929 dollars. This year, 1938, our national income has been
estimated at from $55,000,000,000 to $60,000,000,000 in current dollars, or from $61 to $66 billions in 1929 dollars.

This simply means that average per capita income, or average
per family income, today or in the best year of 1937 has been
much less than it was 13 to 15 years ago. If there is any one
yardstick to measure the extent of recovery more convincingly
than any other this must be it. This for the reason that it is a
composite of all yardsticks. It does not measure improvement
in sale of gasoline alone, or cigarettes alone, or foreign trade
alone. Total national income combines all other indexes.

Every one who loves this country would like to see the
$90,288,000,000 income we should have had, if we had done no
better but just as well *per capita* as we were doing in 1923-25.
But this denies us the benefit of all improvements of science,
technology, and power since then. With them we should today
have a national income with dollars at the same price level, of
$100,000,000,000. Instead we have today 61 to 66 billion
dollars.

Consequently, the man on the shore watching the course of
the ship and having an interest in the cargo has, I think, the just

right to conclude that from the standpoint of recovery the second and third New Deal has not succeeded. He has the right to ask if the ship is not off its course.

We had more prosperity per capita and per family in 1923-25 than we have now. We had that prosperity then without attacking the Supreme Court, without reorganizing the government to give one man practically autocratic power, without emasculating Congress, without going in debt (but instead paying $1,000,000,000 annually on the war debt), without crushing taxation, without destroying the States, without dictating labor relations, without fixing wages and prices by statute, without plowing up cotton, without allocating credit, without W.P.A., P.W.A., F.E.R.A., C.C.C., N.R.A., A.A.A., etc.

1923-25 was not perfect. There were evils in finance, banking and speculation, although they did not reach their rank growth until four or five years later when the crash came. Some of the prosperity of that period, too, was financed by foreign loans which went to protest and nevertheless 1923-25 is the government's own "par." If there is any period since before the World War that is fairly normal, this was it.

The inventory, therefore, concludes as follows:

Average national income 1923-24-25
    (1929 dollars) $79,200,000,000
On same per capita (14% increase of population) basis, income in 1938 should be.... $90,288,000,000

But $90,288,000,000 is still less than we are entitled to. It gives no effect to the benefit of the advance in science, technology and power, which formerly ran some 3 per cent per year. With these benefits, 1938 income should be at least $100,000,000,000.

Instead 1938 income actually is estimated at 61 to 66 billion dollars. Compared to par, we have a 61 to 66 per cent prosperity.

All this leads the man on the shore to ask if the 1923-25 brand (deficient as it was!) of constitutional government and private competitive enterprise was not better than present collectivist dogmas. The latter have demonstrably *not* given us the more abundant life.

It is plain that a more equitable distribution of wealth is not our *prime* need. That may have been—I think was—the prime need in 1923-25. It is important today but it is secondary. Our prime need today is *more wealth*.

Why are we where we are? Why should we have in 1938, nine years after the collapse, only a *61 to 66 per cent prosperity*?

We have:

1. A credit base almost inexhaustible.
2. Banks free from failures, their deposits guaranteed.
3. An industrial plant in need of modernization; obsolescence everywhere.
4. An enormous housing shortage, enough to keep men in the building and material trades at work for ten years just to catch up.
5. Utilities far behind. They could spend at least a billion a year in new construction, for years to come.
6. Railroads needing enough new equipment to keep the plants busy for years.
7. *Not too many* skilled workmen; a shortage, in fact.
8. Still we have billions of idle dollars; millions of idle men. Why?

The answer, as I see it, is that two great systems for managing the *production* of wealth in America are now in conflict—Federal Socialism, or Fascism, and private enterprise. The struggle is on. Neither has won or lost the field. The issue is not yet decided. It is in doubt.

Because it is in doubt the production of wealth is halted. Private enterprise is confronted with "millions of cautions." It is like an automobile attempting to go forward with its brakes set. It hesitates about new ventures—especially long-term commitments. For the first six months of 1938 new capital issues went to the lowest point in three years, and at no time has new capital been more than a fraction of the 1920-1930 figures. All boats are keeping close to shore.

Enterprise does not know what wages the government will compel it to pay; what the government will take from it in taxes; whether government ownership or the sit-down strike will leave it in possession of its own property; whether government will compete with and destroy it. Confronted with all these doubts and fears, it trims sail.

Secretary Morganthau was entirely correct last November when he said we need to promote "the full driving force of private capital."

Instead, the government has further invaded the field of enterprise, and we have a 60 per cent prosperity. We would not have even that except for spending money we do *not* have.

This issue cannot long remain undecided. Either we must go "forward" to complete Fascism, or *wholeheartedly,* and *soon,* return to competitive private enterprise and constitutional democracy.

CHAPTER 26

THE BASIC PROBLEM

"The first principle of human society is "the guarantee to everyone of a free exercise of his industry and the possession of the fruits acquired by it."

—Jefferson.

"This asking for help from government for everything should be deprecated. It destroys the old and worthy sturdy principle of American life which existed in the beginning when men succeeded by their own efforts. This is what has led to the follies of the protective tariff and other laws to that end by which men seek to protect themselves from competition. Never before did I realize the rightfulness of the movement we stand for *and to which all must flock* if they will save themselves and save American civilization. What we need is peace, business peace. Let us have it and the people will work out their own salvation."

—Louis D. Brandeis.

It is hard to know whether it is a greater mistake to over-simplify or over-complicate our problems. My correspondence, however, indicates that people generally are confused and oppressed with what appears to be the enormous complexity of these problems. Many feel that they cannot hope to understand them and therefore make no effort to understand. From this comes a feeling of hopelessness and discouragement. From this comes also the failure to take any part in the formation of public opinion.

Knowing that our problems are immensely difficult, knowing

there is no single or simple solution, I am nevertheless led to believe that we should first attempt to discover the mouth of the river before exploring its tributaries. As Justice Holmes would say, "Let us strike for the jugular." With this explanation I venture to say that the goal of liberalism is not hard to state, however difficult it has been throughout the centuries to achieve that goal. As I view it the goal very simply is a free market place. Let this be demonstrated.

Man prospers honestly only by producing goods (wheat, iron, automobiles, etc.) or by rendering services. He may do so for himself or for others or for both. For example, a farmer may produce milk for his family and for the market. In primitive society the effort to create new wealth is so difficult to those who undertake it that the result is meager,—the standard of living is poor. This is because every man is compelled to depend upon himself for nearly everything. It means that he must often spend a very large amount of energy and time in doing some necessary thing at which he is not expert. As an example; consider Robinson Crusoe making an umbrella. How he agonized over that. He was "all thumbs." It took so much time and effort that he had to neglect other work at which he was skilled. But suppose another sailor had been shipwrecked with him, an expert umbrellaman. Then Robinson could build huts, his shipmate umbrellas, and each could have both huts and umbrellas. Each would thus benefit by the other's skill.

But Robinson Crusoe working alone finds his standard of living very low. The necessities of his situation prevent him from doing the thing for which he has a "knack." He is therefore "jack-of-all-trades and master of none." This fact and this result are as plain as a pikestaff in all times and places where each family lived a self-contained economy. No one who ever supported himself on a Vermont farm could fail to see this. A disproportionate maximum of human energy goes into a minimum result.

As labor was the curse of Adam, the division of labor is the greatest boon the sons of Adam and the daughters of Eve have ever found upon this globe. It is the master key to progress. It unlocks all doors.

With it the blacksmith sets up his shop and does nothing but blacksmithing; the miller erects his waterwheel, the fisherman goes to sea, the lumberjack to the forest, the shepherd to the hill, the farmer to the field, the miner to the tunnel, the teacher to the school, the editor to the sanctum, the doctor to the bedside, the chemist to the test tube, the artist to the canvas.

The division of labor frees every talent. It releases every skill. It unleashes the dynamic, restless, creative, mysterious and unpredictable human soul. It gave us Edison, Burbank, Wright, Bessemer, Pupin, Westinghouse, Goethals. It permits each to exchange his skill for his fellow's skill and to further develop his own. It lifts mankind from the lowest common denominator of universal drudgery to the higher levels of knack, aptitude, skill, talent, and genius. With it and with it alone come commerce, industry, art, science, education, the march of empire, civilization itself.

This beneficent result of the division of labor has taken man from the cave and the jungle and set him on the farms and cities of a civilized society. But it all depends upon its corollary, a free market place where men may exchange their skills with each other upon terms mutually satisfactory. Civilization has grown around the market place. And the progress of civilization has depended upon the degree of freedom of the market.*

To serve the market place, to make it more free, man invented measures of size, weight, length, quantity, and quality. He built ships, wharves, wagons, roads, canals, the iron horse,

* There are of course necessary restrictions to this freedom. It does not, for example, include the freedom to use false weights. Restrictions against cheating, however, enlarge the freedom of those for whose benefit the restriction is imposed. As Abraham Lincoln once said, "When the shepherd drives the wolf from the flock the wolf may say that his freedom is restricted. But it assures the freedom of the flock to live." It is the old balance of "liberty under law."

telegraph, telephone, radio, airplane. He set up banks, warehouses, elevators, refrigerators. He dug for gold and silver. He created money. He invented credit, promissory notes, bills of exchange. He devised mechanisms of international exchange and negotiated commercial treaties between nation and nation. He did all of these things chiefly for the one purpose to bring goods to and from the market place and there to facilitate their exchange. In short, he did all this to exchange his labor with the labor of his fellows, whether of his community, his nation, or the world.

To the degree that the market place is free, men are freed from drudgery. Each does, grows, or makes what he can do *best* and shares that *best* with his fellow's *best*. So the standard of living goes up. When anything prevents or retards this free exchange the standard of living falls. There are many examples. When robber barons levied tribute on the caravans moving along the trade routes of Europe to "Indus and to Ind" the products of East and West could not be exchanged, or only at a premium. Due to the toll taken by the robber less of the goods reached their natural market. The price rose, fewer honest men were able to obtain the goods, and so the standard of living of honest men fell. The standard of living of honest men is more important than that of robbers. The honest man gives something for what he gets and the world is richer. The robber gives nothing and the world is poorer. One adds to, the other subtracts from, the wealth of the world.

In modern times we see the same principle at work when war cuts off trade. Everybody then is forced to get along with little, or with substitutes or the second best. People go without adequate food, heat, or clothing. When trade is thus cut off, instead of prosperity, bustling markets, loaded freight cars, we see high prices, idle ships moored to their wharves, privation, even the slow starvation of millions, as took place during the World War.

Somewhere here is to be found the key to the puzzle of

poverty in a land of enormous natural resources, technology, science, and power. It is a puzzle which the masses cannot understand and the result of which they are rightfully unwilling to accept. We have millions of idle men. We are told they will always be idle,—the willing worker as well as the bum. It is a philosophy of defeat and despair. It is not American. One simply will not believe that these millions of idle men cannot make products useful to each other and so employ each other. We have land enough, capital, resources, men, managerial skill, inventive genius enough to produce plenty for all. Until recent decades the problem of producing enough had not been solved. Famine was an unconquered scourge. But today science so fertilizes soil, improves seed, conquers insects and the diseases of plant life that our food problem is not one of insufficient production—we have in fact an unsaleable surplus. It is a new thing in the world. We have not had time to solve it and so we are paying hundreds of millions of dollars to prevent the surplus from getting larger in a land where millions do not have enough.

The major problem therefore must be the problem of distribution;—the free market place. Of course we need more and more production, for this adds to our wealth, but the immediate Gordian knot to cut is distribution. All kinds of barriers have grown up to restrict the free exchange of goods. Tariffs, land monopoly, suppression of patents, trusts, combinations to artificially hold up prices and limit production, and the control of credit. Together they are like dried grease in an axle. The wheels turn not at all or with difficulty. Sticky costs, inflexible wage scales and debt charges, increasing and inflexible taxes, price fixing, etc., have gummed the gears of distribution.

The collector of taxes has become the greatest middleman in history. He, too, prevents the free exchange of goods. He holds producer and consumer far apart. He collects a huge tribute on all goods passing to market. If automobiles and houses and their constituent parts were wholly free of tax, how many more would be sold? Hundreds of thousands, perhaps millions. How many more men would be employed making them? And producing their steel, rubber, glass, brick, shingles, furniture? In fact there are fewer indictments against collectivism more serious than this. The toll is not less than a fifth to a quarter of consumer cost. In some cases, like cigarettes, the government in effect takes one pack from every two. Government gets more from tobacco than the farmer who grows it; from industrial corporations more than the stockholders.

As practically all taxes are charged to the final consumer and he therefore has less to spend for other goods, we have in taxes, cost and waste of government, one of the main reasons for present unemployment. Reduce taxes and you reduce costs, increase sales and so put men to work. Taxes never made a nation rich since the world began. Do you know of any such case? For the first time in our history we are slowly getting poorer. We are eating our seed corn—consuming our capital.

The barriers to impede the free exchange of goods have been building for a long time. It is not the responsibility alone of any party or any president. They originated chiefly in tariff policies which began a century ago. It is too late now to undo overnight the protective tariff system. The country accepted it and we have built part of our economy upon it. We have, however, carried it too far and particularly so since the end of the World War. The two post-war tariffs and the reprisals they provoked abroad are responsible in large part for the oncoming of the world-wide depression in 1929.

As a simple illustration, we could grow coffee in the United States under the glass roofs of hot-houses, but it would be expensive coffee. Few people would be able to drink it and our standard of living with respect to coffee would fall. We can perhaps produce rubber from goldenrod but it will be a high priced rubber and because the price is high, fewer people will be able to buy it and the standard of living will fall.

We are setting up barriers between state and state of the

Union, taxes on commodities competing locally, inspection laws, etc., all to create state and regional monopolies and so hinder the exchange of goods. We are becoming little Americans.

There is a statesman in the city of Washington. His name is Cordell Hull. More clearly than any man of our times he has seen what these arbitrary restrictions upon the exchange of goods in international trade are doing to us and to the world. He realizes that as natural trade vanishes, as it becomes more and more difficult to get goods, more and more regimentation seems to be the only answer. In the same way the commander of a besieged garrison with limited food supplies is forced to restrict and allot rations to his garrison. Mr. Hull sees what all this will do to democracy here and throughout the world. He sees very plainly that you cannot have free government without a free market. He sees that democracy cannot survive if its price is poverty. He sees that you cannot have world peace when men are kept from food, from raw materials. As a result, Secretary Hull, without fanfare or headlines, has been moving toward plenty, prosperity and peace. No one needs to defend all of the provisions of the different reciprocal trade agreements which have been negotiated. Errors have no doubt been made (for example, the dairy industry may have been prejudiced) but on the whole the future of free government in this country depends upon the success of the effort to free the market place.

Other policies have been put in effect diametrically opposed to Mr. Hull's philosophy. As he would free the market place they would control the market place. As he would increase production they would restrict production. As his policies would inevitably lead to greater volume and lower prices, thus increasing demands for goods and the numbers of those employed in producing them, these contradictory policies lead to higher prices, restricted production, restricted employment, more relief, more W.P.A., more debt, more taxation, more uncertainty, all breaking the courage and morale of the nation. If we were not robbing the children's bank by adding to the national debt, we would be back to 1933.

Because these other policies have prevailed we have statutory limitations on the production of food, coal, cloth, credit, transportation, labor, etc. All this is in the interest of artificially raising prices and wages to a point where millions cannot buy. We constantly legislate for the producer, seldom if ever for the consumer. But we are all consumers or would increasingly be so in a free market place.*

We have attempted to offset industrial price fixing and monopolies with statutory price fixing and monopolies. Rather than predicate our entire national policy upon freeing the market place where the distribution of goods can proceed without tolls or tribute being collected by any one who does not render a useful service, we have attempted at Washington with a gigantic bureaucracy to control but thus perpetuate these tolls collected by one group from all other groups. We have offset one subsidy with a second subsidy. "Equal subsidies for all, special privileges for every one." It is a motto with a strange device. We have tried to heat the room by boiling the thermometer.

We have attempted to transfer economic function from Wall Street to Washington, putting the reins in the hands of the politician. So government undertakes to guarantee wage levels, fix prices, socialize losses, adjust and readjust the economic mechanism, oil the squeaky joints, and out of this, if continued, there can be one result only—a species Fascism.

Mr. Roosevelt himself, when governor, forewarned of this result. He said—

* In this, I am not to be understood as opposed to the Federal Congress exercising its constitutional responsibility to "coin money, regulate the value thereof, and of foreign coin" in the interest of softening the peaks and valleys of the economic curve, known as prosperity and depression. On the contrary, within the margins of human capacity, I think *every effort should be made along this line*. It is one species of regulation which government can alone perform. The present argument deals only with special legislation by pressure groups to protect themselves from the competition of the market.

"Any national administration attempting to make all of the laws for the whole nation would inevitably result in a dissolution of the nation itself."

Later, when president, January 3, 1936, Mr. Roosevelt made a similar warning:

"In thirty-four months we have built up new instruments of public power. In the hands of a people's government this power is wholesome and proper but in the hands of the political puppets of an economic autocracy such powers would provide shackles for the liberties of the people."

The essential difference between Jefferson in distributing power and Mr. Roosevelt in concentrating power, is that Jefferson knew there was no assurance that power would always be "in the hands of a people's government."

Out of this confusion, contradictory policies and conflicting purposes between an effort to control the market and to free the market, we have after six years of the New Deal, practically as many men unemployed as in 1933.

We have been trying to lift ourselves by our bootstraps. By statutes we have sought to protect large groups from competition. N.R.A., while it contained many good features, on the whole resulted in destroying competition and subsidizing monopoly by tolls collected from consumers. The one prolonged spurt of prosperity we have had began when N.R.A. was held unconstitutional. The Supreme Court saved the New Deal from itself for the time being. In February 1937, the attack on the Court, and the attitude of the administration toward the sit-down strike frightened business managers and investors and the second New Deal had its second depression.

We should bend every effort to do nationally what Secretary Hull is attempting to do internationally. As Justice Brandeis has so well said—

"No system of regulation can safely be substituted for the operation of individual liberty as expressed in competition. . . . My idea of the solution of the present day economic trouble is not to stop competition and regulate monopoly, but rather to stop monopoly and regulate competition. . . . With our immense capital available and with the greater capital that is in the brain of the American people we can rely upon a reasonable price and a good article as long as the avenues of competition are kept open. This result cannot be secured by monopoly and price regulation. It is utterly impossible. Progress, advance in methods, invention, all these stand still when competition's spur no longer pricks. This is industrial history."

Similarly, the Federal Trade Commission, in its report in 1934, on the basing point system in the steel industry, said—

"If the capitalistic system does not function as a competitive economy there will be an increasing question whether it can or should endure. *The real friends of capitalism are those who insist on preserving its competitive character.*"

Man is the loser whether paternalism is governmental or corporate. When government exercises economic function the same problems are simply transferred to other hands. The same abuses remain. Real statesmen never confuse Government with God.

A free market is not an unregulated market, as those contend who itch to rule the lives of other men. Every market needs regulation in the public interest. But in a free market competition is the great regulator. It prevents price gouging. It improves quality. It forbids quantity limitation. It gives the consumer most and best for least.

The only other regulator is the policeman. He is personal. Competition is impersonal. The one can be "reached." His judgments can be controlled. We childishly say "pass a law." The Romans were wiser. They said, "Who will watch the watchman?"

With the worst record in the civilized world in dealing with crime we are still crazy enough to want to turn over to more politicians more and more power to control more and more men. In doing so we set up more tribute takers and toll gatherers along more trade routes. We subsidize politics at the expense of business, production, employment.

After seeing enormous tolls collected from the lesser businesses of liquor, race tracks, dance halls, red light districts, prize fighting, wrestling, slot machines, road building, municipal supplies, even school books for our children, we hanker and yearn to place all business, all trade, all agriculture, transportation, banking, mining, etc., under the rule of the politician!

The men who argue for this sort of "control," instead of the competition of the market place, are the New Tories. They are not liberals. They are not progressives. They are taking us straight back to the Old Régime described in Chapter III.

In that chapter I quoted de Tocqueville as to the Toryism of old France. Because the point cannot be too much stressed that the trend today is profoundly reactionary, let me illustrate it further. De Tocqueville wrote in 1856—82 years ago. But 101 years before de Tocqueville, another Frenchmen, Morelly, wrote his Code de la Nature in 1755. Morelly was the 18th century prototype of Mussolini, Hitler, Stalin. He was the economist of the omnipotence of the state, the regulation of all business, and of all persons, the "total absorption of the individual in the body politic." In the ideal society which he would have imposed upon the world he would have it thus: "Nothing belongs wholly to anyone. Property is detestable and anyone who attempts to re-establish it shall be imprisoned for life as a dangerous madman and an enemy to humanity. Every citizen shall be kept and maintained and supplied with work at public expense. All produce shall be gathered in the public granaries to be distributed to citizens for their subsistence. All cities shall be built on the same plan. All private residences shall be alike. All children shall be taken from their families at five years of age and educated together on a uniform plan." This was written

183 years ago, but de Tocqueville writing 82 years ago quoted it as if it were written yesterday.

As one further illustration, I am indebted again to Walter Lippmann's "The Good Society." Louis XIV was a Tory, was he not? What kind of government did he have? Four volumes of 2200 pages were not enough for him to regulate the textile industry. Three more were needed and they did not suffice. In the manufacture of woolens the most minute compulsions were put on the number of threads to the warp. The warp of one manufacturer had to have 1376 threads; another only 1216. The latter was probably a favorite of the ruling politician—the King. Other manufacturers had to "negotiate for four years, from 1730 to 1734, before they could secure permission to use black warp." They never got His Majesty's most gracious consent to weave in black weft. Some competitor, paying a "kick in" to His Majesty, probably had a monopoly of cloth with black weft.

But trade struggles to be free, even at the price of bribery, bootlegging and smuggling. Men will produce goods and sell them—if they can. Life itself depends on it. So there were more regulations and more violations. It is estimated that the effort to control industrial production by French politicians cost the lives of 16,000 persons. They were broken on the wheel, hanged, sent to the galleys, all to protect some vested interest that did not want competition. There was bootlegging in calico, hi-jacking in wool. But trade struggled to be free. It will always struggle to be free, whether in France or Boston harbor filled with tea. But at what a cost in restricted production, *in holding prosperity in low gear,* in denying to the masses the marvelous potentialities for plenty in the present age of power machinery.

At the moment there appears to have been a reversal of attitude from the philosophy of monopoly that led to NRA. President Roosevelt has recommended a study of the problem of monopoly. If this study is conducted with a single desire to ascertain facts and not to burn witches to make a political spectacle it should be welcomed by those who profess allegiance to the competitive system. If conducted in a scientific spirit, despite the temporary inconvenience and uncertainties it will create in business, we may be able to rechart our course in such a way as to prove of enormous value not only to the public but to business itself. From it no perfect solution will come but perhaps a much better one than the present confusion with respect to the Sherman Anti-Trust Act now a half-century old. From it may come a new working hypothesis.

Yes, a *working* hypothesis, one that works for the greatest good of the greatest number. Let us avoid dogmatism, rigid formulas, brittle doctrines. We are dealing with the web on the loom. As Justice Oliver Wendell Holmes once said, "We should allow for some play in the joints of the machine."

When, for example, does bigness become badness? Surely we have passed the time when we will say all bigness is bad. We should examine this question of bigness, combination or consolidation from its *functional* side, rather than from some arbitrary political preconception of size itself. God Almighty made the violet small, the oak tree large. We should try to determine if in this business and that business there is some natural—not artificial—law of growth.

In one business, bigness permits the minute subdivision of overhead, the economies of mass buying and mass production, the ability to maintain costly but necessary departments of research and experiment, the long purse of reserves that carry it over the valleys of depression. If in such business all these advantages of bigness over smallness are constantly passed on in a better product at a lower price, by a management that feels its responsibility of trusteeship for owner, worker, and consumer, then it would seem to be entitled to a favorable verdict in the court of public opinion.

Paying full tribute, as we must, to the initiative, energy and courage of the "little man," his final fate will probably be determined by the realities of economics, rather than by theories of law. Can he "deliver the goods" cheaper and better than the larger aggregation of capital? Does he have efficiencies and economies of his own to overbalance the efficiencies and economies of his greater rival? Where does the large concern run into the law of diminishing economic returns? At what point does its size begin to be a handicap rather than a help? We know of the disease described by medical men as elephantiasis—beef and fat in place of brain and thought. Is there such a thing as economic elephantiasis, when the giant is outrun by the pygmy?

The answer, in the long run, will decide the fate of both giant and pygmy as they compete for the consumer's dollar by offering most and best for least. In automobile manufacture the giant has won. No mechanic, however smart, could hope to produce a car as cheaply as Ford, or General Motors, or Chrysler, or Nash, or the Studebaker—that excellent car made in my home city of South Bend. The consumer, and especially the politician, may both shed tears for the passing of the "little man," but they both buy the goods of the one who gives most for least, whoever that may be, whether the humble "pants presser" or an industrial giant, whether the corner grocery or the chain store.

When bigness, even though wrapped in the flag, and anointed with large and laudable words, has, however, no justification to worker, consumer, and investor through its *mechanics*, but acquires size only to dominate the market, to freeze out its competitors, to issue securities against write-ups, to permit huge underwriting and legal fees, to feed the vanity of the promoters, to deprive investors of a real and effective control, to allow huge salaries and bonuses to insiders, to become, in fact, a "milking machine," it has no justification and in the interest of all business and the survival of democracy itself, it should be ruled off the field of our enterprise.

Even though some economies in finance, and the cost of capital through the diversity of risk and the greater supposed security of farflung business units may flow from bigness, yet if it depends only on alleged or real economies, in the field of *finance*, rather than in the *mechanics* of operation, it cannot win its case at the bar of public opinion. The cost of public ill will and social unrest accruing through these *financial* empires must in the long or short run outweigh any alleged advantages. With respect to this kind of bigness I believe President Roosevelt is unquestionably correct and he and Congress should be supported by business leaders as we set our hands to reconsider this problem.

To the extent that business proves incapable of self-discipline in the interest of the millions, government will occupy new ground. The millions will demand it, and they have the votes. The evils of Big Government will not be less than the evils of Big Business. They will be more.

The masses today know only of the evils of Big Business. Jefferson and his compeers freed them from Big Government so long ago they have forgotten what our fathers learned. Our children will remember what we forgot. I hope they will not have to pay too great a tuition of poverty and suffering to learn the truth that built the western world, that progress comes from emancipation, not coercion.

CHAPTER 27

THE PROGRAM OF LIBERALISM

"Restrain men from *injuring* one another . . . but leave them otherwise *free* to regulate their own pursuits of industry and improvement."

—Jefferson.

"It is not for an abstraction that men have toiled and died. . . . We speak of liberty as one thing, and of virtue, wealth, knowledge, invention, national strength and national independence as other things. But of all these, Liberty is the source, the mother, the necessary condition. She is to virtue what light is to color; to wealth what sunshine is to grain."

—Henry George.

"Liberty is not only a private blessing, it is the vital spring of energy of the state itself."

—Edmund Burke.

Unless all values are twisted "liberalism" still has some connection with "liberty." The great liberals were "liberators";— Jefferson, Lincoln, Mazzini, Bolivar, many others. Liberalism frees men from the toll takers on the world's trade routes,— privilege, slavery, monopoly, "the divine right of kings," and every form of tribute which the State farms out to its favorites and concessionaires in order that they may reap where others sow.

Many collectivists are good men. They adopt collectivism to rid the world of abuses. They think the managers of collectivism will be of purer clay. In the minds of such men, collectivism

231

is a remedy (although liberals consider it a mistaken one) for real abuses.

But these are not the only ones who favor collectivism. It is also favored by those who seek power for power's sake. They want power concentrated in their hands. They then become the greatest toll takers of all time, because the greatest toll is the end of all civil rights, the loss of liberty. It is an unbroken story that in time the power-drunk men of iron take command of every collectivist movement however sincerely designed.

Whatever else may be said of it collectivism is compulsion. Liberalism is emancipation. It frees men from the tyrannies of kings, lords, feudal barons, financial barons, industrial barons. The inventors and scientists are liberals. They free men from superstition, drudgery, disease, ignorance. However sincere collectivists may be, their faces are turned to the past—a dark past. The liberal faces the future.

It is little wonder that the great liberals, in whatever field of action, have generally been deeply religious men. They believed that Truth has to be discovered, not decreed. "Know the Truth and the Truth shall make you free." They believed that man is *in fact* a child of God, not a pawn of the State nor any ruling class therein. Liberals believe that men, *all men,* have certain *inalienable* rights with which they were endowed by their Creator Himself and for which they cannot rightfully be called to account nor made to pay toll. The collectivist on the other hand finally admits no limitation to the exercise of the power of the State. He makes Caesar supreme. For this reason collectivists instinctively recognize a free religion as hostile to their claims. Religion rests its case on the ground that men are not things but persons; that they are not something to be disposed of like cattle.

The main business of liberalism in the past has been, now is, and always must be, to take loads off the backs of men. As Lincoln said: "Weights should be lifted from the shoulders of all men." It is not the main function of liberalism to "take care" of men. Nor to wet nurse or feed them (for their votes). It is to free men so that they can take care of themselves. It is to give them an equal chance and a fair field. It is to give men "the democracy of opportunity and the aristocracy of achievement."

The sincere collectivist believes that liberalism is a cold altar, that only modern Caesars are competent to manage affairs. You may tell these men that this new (?) dogma degrades man from the great and "free and equal" estate that liberalism intended should be his. But in reply they will say that the result is dictated by necessity, that no other hands are strong enough.

Nevertheless the presumption must be in favor of liberty and liberalism. Liberalism has a record behind it. Let us examine it.

In the few decades since men threw shackles down and fetters off, with the political, industrial and economic revolutions initiated by Thomas Jefferson, James Watt, and Adam Smith, men have made greater progress in the attainment of happiness by a larger proportion of human beings than in all previous history. These were the years of the greatest liberty and the greatest prosperity, the greatest tolerance and the least cruelty the world has ever known. It was the age of emancipation. It freed men to do their *best* and exchange it in free markets for the *best* of other men. The United States, for example, has been the greatest free market the world has ever known and it has prospered as it has been free.

I am glad to say that a respectable portion of the New Deal has been in this tradition. I have mentioned Secretary Hull's effort to free and increase trade as an example. But more and more in its later development, the New Deal has grown impatient. It has swung from liberalism to collectivism. It has sought to manage men, not to free them. The Old Deal fostered Big Business and winked at its evils. The second and third New Deal fosters Big Government and winks at its evils. To use the words of Newton Baker, Lewis Douglas, and Leo Wolman:

"The one fostered private monopoly in the name of national prosperity. The other has fostered state controlled monopolies in the name of the national welfare. We believe that both are an aberration from the basic principles upon which this nation has grown great and has remained free."

President Roosevelt has been entirely right in attacking the *evils* of private collectivism. But in promoting governmental collectivism he is choosing the wrong weapon. No prince of privilege, in American history at least, ever held more men in greater dominion than the millions of workers under W.P.A. and all the other government substitutions for opportunity and prosperity. As an emergency, yes. But after six years all of these emergency substitutes are leveling off into a permanent defeatism. When the W.P.A. worker gets his month's check, he is as much of a slave of the government for his vote and next month's pay as any wage slave in industry. *These men are not free men.* And that one fact damns the program as a permanent policy. A dreary, hopeless future—is that all we can offer them? It is all that the apologists of collectivism have offered them,— "bread and circuses."

These advocates of collectivism, not the political machine and bureaucracy which feeds upon it, now say in effect that it was not liberalism which chiefly gave America the greatest century in the annals of time. They say it was "the frontier," the free land of the West, our natural resources of coal, timber, minerals, soil fertility, that were free to the homesteader, the dispossessed, the misfit in old surroundings. It gave them a second chance, a second opportunity.

Great as the frontier was, and profound as the effect of its passing has been on our national life, I am persuaded that it has been overemphasized. Read the story of Luther Burbank, a free man in a free land. He brought to California in his brain more wealth than all its gold and silver from the days of '49. His unpredictable genius has pushed out the frontiers of that state, transforming its farm life from the wheat and wool of the old frontier to the new frontiers of fruit and flower, nut and vegetable, with millions of customers the old frontier never had. Nobody gave Burbank a quota or a government check. But he gave California more wealth than any government or legislature ever did. *Man,* not the state,—"Man, the Unknown," is the creator of all wealth.

It is that type of man which collectivism cannot anticipate, cannot make plans for, except to fit him into the fixed patterns of bureaucracy *and thus prevent his growth.*

The old frontier was limited because geography has boundaries. But the new frontiers of science are as limitless as man's desires. The old frontier was closed by state and national governments about 1890-1900. It was the end of free land. The opening of the Indian Territory was the last great rush to the land. On that day did America come to an end? It did not. Since 1900 we have grown in population by 50 million people. What has supported them? New land?—No, new science. And where are they, on the farm? No, they are at the frontiers of invention. The automobile in one form or another is supporting five million of them. The president of the American Chemical Society says that one-third of factory production was unheard of in 1880. A few years ago General Electric Company announced that 60% of its business was in products not known 10 years previously.

The Mellon Institute of Research, private not governmental, has produced 650 new products and established 10 new industries. It is the liberalism of science working within the liberalism of politics. Long since America is supposed to have come to an end with the closing of the frontier, we have found 10,000 new metal alloys and 250,000 new chemical compounds. *Man,* not the State. Free men seeking to do their best and exchange it in free markets.

Formerly the duPont Company made explosives almost exclusively. Now it is said that 99% of its business is in peacetime commodities. In dyestuffs research it spent 22 million dollars before it made $1 of profit, and another 21 million over a total 18 year period before it recovered its investment. But now American dyes employ thousands of Americans and have made the nation itself practically independent of the world, in peace or in war.

As James Truslow Adams has said in a recent article, to which I am indebted for much of the foregoing—

> "The total number of people who in another decade or two might be living on this new frontier staggers the imagination. . . . An enormous responsibility rests upon all governments. For this frontier which can happily support our future populations may be closed by unwise legislation as readily as by iron doors. And it is not only man's *new* frontier to which he presses eagerly forward but his *last*."

The danger, the great and imminent danger, of collectivism is that it will close these new frontiers by its intermeddling, its constant unsettlement of everything; its unpredictability; its taxation; its new monopolies; its toll taking by political rackets; its war not on privilege but on capital; its stirring up of class antagonism. Let us be very careful about closing these new frontiers to the same kind of men and women who went to the old frontiers. It was initiative, courage and self-reliance that built all we have. It is these qualities alone that can build an even greater future.

If free men with *free access to opportunity* cannot make a maximum of wealth and prosperity, who can? If the sparkplug of the profit motive cannot make the engine go, what can? Outside of the struggle for life itself of the man in the wilderness, there are just two things which cause men to work and nations to prosper, the hope of reward, or the lash of the slave.

Compared with all other systems, the American Way has been the greatest success the world has known. It has come about without compulsion, Fascism, planning from the top. Compared to perfection, the American Way has fallen short.

Our business is to perfect it, not to scrap it!

Let us examine its failures without blinking. This is where many friends of the system are at fault. They do not ask themselves honestly why social unrest exists.

America has more bathtubs than any nation in the world. But this means very little to a family that has no bathtub, wants one, is willing to work for it and still cannot get it. There are some people who do not want bathtubs, at least enough to work for them. They prefer to ride the brake beams from town to town or sit all day on the court house fence while their wives take in washing. If they get a few dollars in their pockets they do not report for work until the money is gone. They are worth little to employers, less to themselves. No legislative body in the history of the world has ever been able to write a law for the lazy. *Shiftlessness is in fact a form of exploitation.* The shirkers are parasites on the backs of the workers, whether they are rich shirkers or poor shirkers.

Our concern must be for those *who want to work* and are willing to give value received. To such a man thrown out of work by a modern labor-saving device and unable to find new employment, it does little good to tell him, as is the fact, that invention and science and machinery have given employment to far more men than they have displaced. He, however, has a personal displacement problem and it should be recognized.

For the family whose income does not provide even adequate food, clothing and shelter, it does little good to say that America as a nation has the greatest income in the world. Behind this social unrest there are genuine wrongs. One of them is an unjust distribution of income and wealth. Many wild statements have been made on this matter such as 2% of the people having 98% of the wealth. Nevertheless there has been and is a wholly inequitable distribution of income.

For authority, I go to a study made by the Brookings Institution, "America's Capacity to Consume." They report that in 1929, our peak year, out of 27,474,000 families, 11,653,000 families (or 42% of the total families) had incomes of less than

$1500 (average for the family $858). Their total income was just under 10 billion dollars. At the other end, the Institution reports that 36,000 families with incomes in excess of $75,000 (average $272,000) had a total income of 9.8 billion or about the same as the other group. "Thus it appears that 0.1% of the families at the top receive practically as much as 42% of the families at the bottom of the scale." The average family income of $858 and $272,000 shows a ratio of 1 to 317.

Making all reasonable allowance for the disparity in human ability; granting the willingness of society to pay a reasonable reward to men of great ability and usefulness—recognizing the necessity for capital accumulations to finance progress, I, for one, accept the conclusion that a disparity of 317 to 1 in average realized income creates entirely too many hazards for democracy.*

In the old days in England and in the American Colonies the law gave the eldest son the entire property of his father and in turn made him a sort of guardian of his younger brothers and sisters. There was also the law of entail under which property could not be disposed of by deed or will but must go down in the same family for all time, whether it bred geniuses or fools. These great abuses of the concentration of wealth were smashed by Thomas Jefferson in the reformation of the law of Virginia.

Similarly, in our time this disparity of 317 to 1 can be reached by proper taxes on income and inheritance, (particularly the latter) and by taxing income from privilege higher than earned income. The rate of tax should, of course, not exceed the peak load that courage and initiative will carry. It should not prevent the production of wealth. We can do whatever is necessary to correct the mal-distribution of wealth without changing the Constitution, destroying the independence of the judiciary,

---

* In order to be perfectly clear, let me say that I am not arguing for equality of income. Equal reward for an unequal contribution violates justice. An unequal reward for an equal contribution does also. But the *large* income seldom depends wholly on the *contribution* of the person. This was made clear fifty years ago by Andrew Carnegie, in his "My Partners, the People."

have nothing to do with the industry of the occupant but come in the form of "unearned increment" on the bare land should be taxed at a higher rate than are improvements, buildings, etc. created by the toil and sweat of the owner. The individual should be entitled within reasonable limits to all the wealth which he creates. Society on the other hand should be entitled to the wealth that society creates, such as the rental value of the bare land. There are no toll gatherers for whom there is less excuse than those families, who generation after generation "toil not neither do they spin," but live on the land rentals created by the industry of others—the community.

The corporation has been described by Nicholas Murray Butler as "the greatest single discovery of modern times." It has been the means by which many small and large investors could pool their capital. Under the rule of limited liability they did not risk anything but their actual investment against the debts of the corporation. This protection, not known to partnerships nor individual businesses, made modern capital available. Without it, modern industry could not have performed its many beneficent miracles. This in turn *freed business from the State,* as previously the only source of large funds was a grant from the sovereign, e.g., from Isabella to Columbus.

But serious abuses have grown up with the corporation,—holding companies performing no useful economic function, stock issues and "split-ups" so numerous and so different in legal result as to become a jungle to screen wholly indefensible practices,—many other sins of omission and commission.

But evil as these abuses have become, it is necessary to point out the simple fact that *the law* created, and can remove the means from which the evils arose. The corporation is a creature of the state; limited liability is a privilege; the right of one corporation to own stock in another corporation (holding company) is a privilege; the right of a corporation to do business in the state of its creation, or in interstate commerce, is a privilege;

the right to issue voting or nonvoting securities and to fix their priorities to income or assets is a privilege.

If from these privileges evils arise, restrict or remove the state-created privilege and you destroy the evil. To the extent that competitive "charter mongering" by the states is an evil, that can be dealt with either by uniform state legislation, or by Federal action.

Again this is the liberal program. It does not set up Big Government as a competitor of Big Business. It does not make the State the sole source of credit and the "master" of all business. It prevents "men from *injuring* one another . . . but leaves them otherwise *free* to follow their own pursuits of industry and improvement."

As we think the matter over, what great evil exists in our economic structure which cannot be fairly and adequately dealt with under the liberal program of private enterprise and constitutional government rather than Fascism or Socialism or Communism—and without the greater evils of these alternatives?

Surely there is nothing in Jeffersonian liberalism that requires natural resources to be wasted; soil fertility to be depleted; slums to exist; or exploitation of one group by another group to continue. No, liberalism was designed for the *very purpose* of making men "free and *equal*" before the law and before the opportunities of a free society. It is not liberalism, or the system of private enterprise or constitutional government as such, any more than the teachings of Christ, which have failed. The failure has been in *men* and not in principles. The failure has been due in large part to *government itself in not protecting these principles,*—a failure which would become more pronounced as collectivism pushes government farther into the field of economic management and ownership.

Take the evil of the hard bargain. The first article of mine ever published was, "What Is a Voluntary Assumption of Risk?" I attacked the hoary legalism that a factory worker may not recover damages for injuries due to defective machinery, etc., when he knew of the defect. The doctrine was that he voluntarily assumed the risk and must, if hurt, go the rest of his life minus his hand or leg or eye, and without any compensation. I asked what is *voluntary* about a man accepting employment and the risk of defective machinery when he or his wife or children *are hungry*. He cannot wait. Inequality in "waiting power" is something democracy must recognize.

Now that evil, and dozens like it, have been cured *without the State taking over the factory and operating it*. It has been cured by removing the advantage *the law itself* had given the employer.

So the right of collective bargaining is necessary to prevent unfair advantage being taken of the necessities of the individual worker. Make men *"free and equal,"*—capital under its managers and labor under its own leaders, and you make State factories wholly unnecessary.

Nor is there any reason why liberalism cannot adequately deal with the problem of the man displaced from the pay roll by a labor-saving machine. That risk to the individual worker can be reasonably insured against in the same way that we have dealt with similar risks under our workmen's compensation and employers' liability laws. They have been charged to the cost of the operation, as a risk against which society itself should pay premiums.

The importance of security for savings,—banks, building and loan associations, insurance companies, etc., cannot be overestimated. It is one of the saddest features of panics and depressions that so much is lost by thrifty, self-denying and hardworking people who struggle *to take care of themselves*. But it is not necessary for government to own and operate banking or insurance, or be the sole source of credit. In fact it has now become a question whether the extravagance of government may not be the greatest of all threats to savings.

One thing the government can alone do and should do. This

is to do *whatever can be done* to prevent too violent changes in the underlying price level. Our fathers gave Congress power to deal with this vital problem. No new power is necessary.

Space prevents further illustrations. The program is incomplete. Everyone may add to it. Nor can any such program be made final. The march of science constantly creates new problems requiring new solutions.

But I shall be sorry indeed if these very inadequate paragraphs do not present these questions to a fair and candid mind: Is it necessary for the modern State to take over business in order to cure the evils of business? *Will collectivism cure these evils?* Will it not create even *greater* evils?

◇

Abraham Lincoln once said, "We shall nobly save or meanly lose the last best hope of earth,"—a society of free men, equal before the law and with equal right at the doors of opportunity. "Equal rights for *all;* special privileges for *none.*"

If this "last best hope of earth" is saved, its salvation will come only from *men and women.* How can there be a "social conscience" without a personal conscience? Programs are futile in themselves. "Liberalism" cannot save America, but liberal and just men and women can.

It was not government that overthrew slavery; it was Wilberforce and Wendell Phillips and William Lloyd Garrison and Harriet Beecher Stowe. It was not the thirteen Colonies that wrote the Declaration of Independence, it was Jefferson. It was not the Chief Executive who spoke at Gettysburg; it was Lincoln.

What caused free enterprise to be so discredited in the public mind? Is it not that too often men in positions of great responsibility, whether in public or private life, forget that every position is a *public trust.* A deserved confidence is the "priceless ingredient." It is beyond the State to confer. You cannot incorporate character. You cannot legislate justice. But without them no system of free enterprise, or free government can

succeed. When these are gone, there is only one thing left—
Force. There can be no bricks without straw; no prosperous
nation without industrious men and women; no great State
without great citizens.

Men are beginning to say all over America that the *real
problem* is a revival of the human spirit, which was wrung hard
and dry by the World War. Call this religion if you please.
I believe it to be profoundly true. We need statesmen in industry more than legislation. We need men in public life who will
at every hazard stand by their guns on fundamental questions.

Men lose faith in banks when they lose faith in *bankers*. They
lose faith in private capitalism when its *managers* break faith.
When *public officials* are no longer trusted, nor respected, democracy and free government are no longer trusted, nor respected. Every failure of character brings the new Caesars closer.
The one thing that can prevent their coming is that all men,
but particularly those in positions of responsibility and leadership, develop a code that certain things simply *"aren't done,"*—
the *noblesse oblige* of democracy. We have had, still have, that
kind of men.

I do not say that men are more important than principles.
Nevertheless men in the mass do not follow programs. They
follow men. If these men are worthy of trust, *they will be
trusted*, and the principles *they* believe in will be believed in,
also.

There is not a public official, business executive, leader of
labor or agriculture, or any American anywhere who can shoulder off onto the State *his* responsibility to be fair, decent, generous and just. This "last best hope on earth" depends on *him*.

Call it what you will. If the Golden Rule seems shopworn,
call it "the square deal," call it sportsmanship, decency, justice,
kindness. In the long run, its "absence makes all prosperities
valueless, its presence, all hardships endurable."

CHAPTER 28

"TO OURSELVES AND OUR POSTERITY"

"If in the opinion *of the people* the *distribution* or modification of the *constitutional power* be in any particular wrong, let it be corrected by an amendment in the way which the Constitution designates.

"But let there be *no change by usurpation;* for though this in one instance may be the instrument of good, *it is the customary weapon by which free governments are destroyed.* The precedent must always greatly overbalance in permanent evil any partial or transient benefit which the use can at any time yield."

—Washington's Farewell Address.

"Stand with anybody that stands right. Stand with him while he is right and part with him when he goes wrong."

—Abraham Lincoln.

As one reads and rereads the story of those who laid the foundations of our Republic, the more one is impressed with the immense pride they took in their work. It was an honest and selfless pride. These men were gazing down long vistas. They were thinking of "posterity." No father walking with his young son, no mother fondling at her breast her little child, ever had a greater hope. The Declaration of Independence and the Constitution of the United States—how they hoped these truths would endure, would spread their blessing throughout the entire world. In the speeches they made, in the letters they exchanged with one another, one can see plainly an anxiety almost paternal, a hope almost sublime.

I am not ashamed to say that I revere these men,—particularly Jefferson and his *dream*, Washington and his *character*. I am certain that men never lived who lived more gallantly, or did work more honest and strong. I am one of their "posterity." It was for *me*, as it was for *you*, that they spoke in such large accents.

What these men were building was a "new order of the ages." Yes, *"of the ages."* They were safeguarding the *"inalienable"* rights of man, rights which no government could lawfully seize, no majority vote away. These rights they intended "posterity" to have—you, and your children. The greatest of these rights was liberty. The greatest danger to liberty was the concentration of power. Its greatest safeguard was the distribution of power.

It is true that they provided a method for amending their work. But it is plain that they never had it in mind that the *basic principles of free government* which they set on parchment were to be changed. They knew, of course, that they would be helpless to prevent it if the time ever came when, as President Washington wrote La Fayette, there should no longer "remain any virtue in the body of the people."

Their anxiety was not that the basic principles were not correct, but that the people might not remain steadfast. They knew it was only a *great* people who could save a *great* government.

But whatever amendment by way of detail or mechanics the future might deem wise, it is certain that they never dreamed that far reaching changes in the Constitution's distribution of power would be made without submitting the question honestly and directly to the people. And certainly they could never have dreamed that these changes would ever be justified by the claim of a "mandate" from a majority acting under the mass-psychology of a great depression, and under *money pressure from government itself*.

If the American people want the states destroyed; if they want all power centered in Washington, and that power cen-ered in the Executive; if they prefer auctions to elections, and sycophants to citizens; in short, if they want a species of Fascism to supplant the government of Washington, Jefferson and Lincoln, and if they so express themselves *freely, deliberately and constitutionally,* their decision must be accepted, however much one might regret it.

But consider a moment. Except to re-legalize liquor, not a *single* constitutional amendment has been proposed by the present administration in the past six years by which the people *themselves* could decide—and do so freely—upon these profound changes, or *any one of them,* on the merits of a stated proposition.

In fact, President Roosevelt in his speech of March 9, 1937, on the Supreme Court packing bill, said not only that it was difficult to draw an amendment to change our form of government to his heart's desire, or to get Congress to agree to submit it, but that, if drawn and submitted, the States might *constitutionally reject it!* And because the States—the people—might reject it, he would accomplish his purpose in *some other way.*

If in the next five, ten or fifteen years this dark tide of constitutional immorality sweeps away this "last best hope of earth," what will our "posterity" think of *us?*

Millions of Americans of both the great parties do not approve the new European "purge" introduced into our politics; nor the silent purchase of the destruction of the States, their communities and citizens. They do not like the intolerance that has crept into public life—on both sides. They dislike men who, for votes and power, fan the flames of class hatreds rather than try to conciliate groups and adjust social equities. They resent the destruction of the freedom and character of millions by the use of billions. They witness with profound anxiety the degrading level under which appeals for votes are now being made. They know their "posterity"—their children—will some day have to pay the bill, *financial and moral!*

These millions of men and women, followers of Washington,

followers of Jefferson, followers of Lincoln, prefer this Union of States to a bureaucratic empire; constitutional democracy to one-party rule; an independent judiciary, with its faults, to one-man rule, with his faults; private enterprise, regulated in the public interest—to Socialism, Communism or Fascism.

But fundamentally, and in the last analysis, their great objection is that we are emasculating if not actually destroying the Constitution of Washington, Jefferson and Lincoln. The "consent of the governed" from which all "just powers" of government are derived, a consent, *freely* given, and *constitutionally* given, is denied them.

I close with *Jefferson—The Forgotten Man:*

> "To take a single step beyond the boundaries thus specifically drawn around the powers of Congress, is to take possession of a boundless field of power, no longer susceptible of any definition."

"A boundless field of POWER." They have that in Europe today.

THE END